A Bible Storybook Celebrating the Greatest Storyteller of All

THE STORYTELLER'S BIBLE

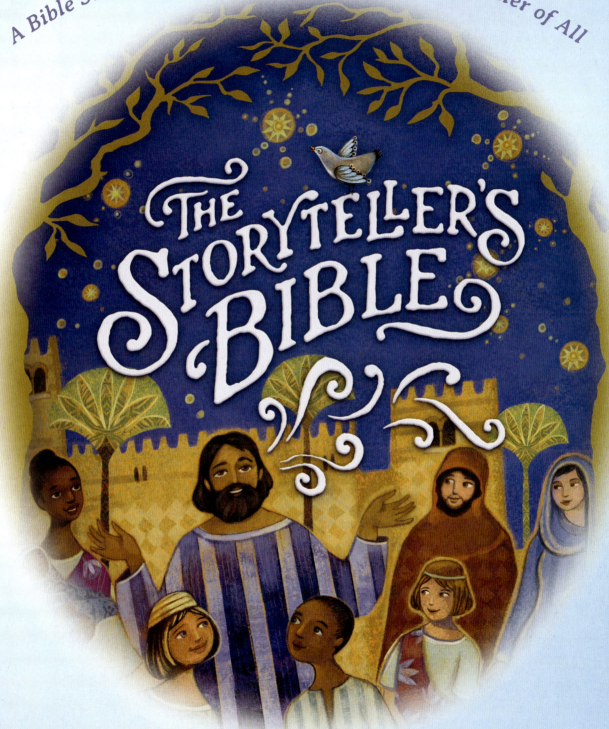

Kathryn Butler

To Jack and Christie—
Harbor the Story in your heart, always.

Published in 2025 by B&H Publishing Group, Brentwood, Tennessee.
Text and illustrations copyright © 2025 by B&H Publishing Group.
Kathryn Butler is represented by Wolgemuth & Wilson.
ISBN: 979-8-3845-0306-4
Scripture quotations are taken from The Holy Bible, English Standard Version®
Copyright © 2001 by Crossway Bibles, a publishing ministry of Good News Publishers.
Scriptures are also taken from the Christian Standard Bible®, Copyright © 2017 by
Holman Bible Publishers. Used by permission. Christian Standard Bible® and CSB® are
federally registered trademarks of Holman Bible Publishers.
Dewey Decimal Classification: C220.95
SUBHD: BIBLE—STORIES / BIBLE—READING / GOSPEL
Printed in Shenzhen, Guangdong, China, November 2024
1 2 3 4 5 6 • 29 28 27 26 25

Contents

Note to Grown-Ups 5

Let Me Tell You a Story 6

1. In the Beginning 8
2. The Curse in the Garden 16
3. The Great Flood 24
4. The Tower to the Sky 32
5. The Promise in the Stars 38
6. The Ram in the Thicket 46
7. A Brother Betrayed 52
8. The Fire in the Bush 60
9. Storms, Swarms, and Deep, Deep Darkness 68
10. A Sea Divided 76
11. The Wilderness 82
12. The Trumpets and the Tumbling Wall 90
13. The Shepherd King 96
14. The Cries of the Prophets 104
15. In the Belly of the Fish 112
16. The Fiery Furnace 118
17. Stone by Stone 124
18. The Savior in the Manger 132
19. Royal Gifts and a Flight to Egypt 140
20. The River and the Dove 148
21. Temptation in the Wilderness 154

22.	The Wondrous Teacher	162
23.	The Prodigal Son	170
24.	Miraculous Healings	176
25.	Bread to Feed Thousands	184
26.	The Storm That Hushed	192
27.	Glory on a Mountaintop	198
28.	Lazarus Raised	204
29.	The King on the Donkey	210
30.	Tears in the Garden	216
31.	The Terrible Betrayal	224
32.	The Darkest Day	230
33.	The Empty Tomb	236
34.	Into the Clouds	242
35.	Tongues of Flame	248

Ten Tips for Reading Aloud 254

Pointing Children to the Gospel Through Great Stories 258

After "The End" 262

About the Artists 266

About the Author 272

Note to Grown-Ups

Something wondrous occurs when we read stories to children.

Research tries to quantify the magic. Just twenty minutes of read-aloud time a day, studies proclaim, nurture literacy and cognitive development.[1] Yet those of us privileged to crack open a book with a child see something more. Something enchanting.

We glimpse it as kids plead for one more chapter, or as they snuggle closer when the hero plunges into danger. We see it as they lean forward in anticipation, wondering if Charlotte will save Wilbur, or if Eustace will ever escape his dragonish fate. When we read stories to children, before our eyes we see truths inspire their minds and shape their hearts. As author Kate DiCamillo so poignantly states, "We let our guard down when someone we love is reading us a story. We exist together in a little patch of warmth and light."[2]

The Storyteller's Bible invites grown-ups and children to linger together in that warmth and light through a retelling of the greatest story of all—the true story. The story of how our loving, all-powerful God took on flesh, dwelt among us, and laid down His life so we might live.

The following pages include thirty-five Bible stories selected to offer kids a cohesive retelling of the gospel narrative. Each story takes about five minutes to read, intentionally brief for sharing during the lull before Sunday school dismissal or in the drowsy minutes before bed. You can pluck out stories in isolation, but because the book is written as one overarching narrative, children might glean the most if they hear the stories successively, like chapters from a children's novel.

As you read, you'll find call-out questions in bold that can prompt discussion with your listeners. "More of the Story" questions at the end of each story prompt kids to look up Bible verses for those moments with older listeners eager to learn more. If time allows, pause in your readings to elicit kids' thoughts and invite them to ponder and delight.

May these stories spark wonder in children's hearts, engage their minds, and point them to the greatest Storyteller of all—the Storyteller who, through Christ, offers us the brightest and most beautiful of happy endings.

Kathryn Butler

---

[1] John S. Hutton, Tzipi Horowitz-Kraus, Alan L. Mendelsohn, et al. "Home Reading Environment and Brain Activation in Preschool Children Listening to Stories." *Pediatrics* 136 no. 3 (2015), 466-478.

[2] Meghan Cox Gurdon. *The Enchanted Hour: The Miraculous Power of Reading Aloud in the Age of Distraction*. Harper Collins (New York), 2019, xiii.

Let Me Tell You a Story . . .

Do you have a favorite story? What makes it so special?

Does it feature a brave hero who triumphs against overwhelming odds?

Do monsters and marvels spring from the pages?

Do characters trek through mysterious lands dappled in color and mist?

Do valiant warriors fight against the powers of darkness, or do knights clad in gleaming armor save damsels trapped in towers?

Does your heart thrill when you read or hear of such glittering things?

There's a reason great stories linger with us long after we've read "THE END." Stories teach and inspire us. They invite us to consider what may be and to remember the wonders of old. They train us to run toward what is good, beautiful, and lovely . . . and to run *away* from what lurks in the shadows.

And best of all, the *greatest* stories point to the most wonderful story of all: the story of a terrible curse that gripped a once shimmering land. The story of a people desperate for rescue and a radiant, all-loving Hero who gave up everything to save those He loved.

Read on, and journey into the greatest story. The best story. The story that belongs to you, to me, and to every person on every corner of this shining, windswept earth.

This story has the power to change minds and hearts. And best of all, this story is TRUE. It is the story of the depth and breadth and height of God's love for you.

Read on, dear friend. Read on, delight, and hold tight to the wonders that unfold.

Illustrations by Monica Garofalo

In the Beginning

Genesis 1-2; Job 38; Psalm 104; John 1:1-5; Acts 17:25

Many great stories begin with, "Once upon a time." *This* story starts before time began.

It begins before you were born, before your parents met, and even before your great-great-great-great grandfather took his first breath.

It begins long before peanut butter and storybooks, swing sets, hot cocoa, and sandcastles at the beach. Seahorses didn't yet bob in the ocean. No porcupines nosed through brambles, and no sparrows yet graced the air with their song.

No mountains arched up their backs like cats after a long nap. Rain didn't glaze any rooftops, rivers didn't flow, and no sunshine or moonbeams set the sky aglow.

In the beginning, all was dark and empty. Nothing that we now see or touch or hear existed.

Close your eyes. Can you imagine what this must have been like?

In all that nothingness, God was there. God was *everywhere*, with His Spirit hovering over the darkness. And in the darkness and emptiness of the beginning, He drew up a plan to give us life and breath and everything. He wrote the very first story—*our* story. And all that He wrote was good.

"Let there be light!" God commanded, and at His word, light burned through the darkness. God gathered the light, called it day, and separated it from the darkness, which He called night. Upon His word the very first day blazed into being.

God wasn't done weaving His story. He stretched out the heavens and studded them with glittering suns and planets and galaxies that swept stardust into their arms. He pooled the waters into the oceans and laid the foundation of the earth, heaping stone into mountains and sculpting magnificent canyons. The stars sang for joy as He worked.

But still, God wasn't done. Like the gentlest of gardeners, He coaxed plants from the soil. At His word, grasses whipped in the wind, flowers burst into bloom, and trees shaded the earth with canopies of leaves. Then He fastened the sun and the moon into the sky to march out the days and illuminate all He'd made.

But still, God wasn't done! He filled the sparkling blue ocean with life: whales and sharks, octopuses and fish, crabs and waving sea anemones.

He filled the vast blue sky with birds of all kinds: hummingbirds and screech owls, starlings and eagles, and cardinals and flamingos in the colors of the sunset.

Finally, at God's command, land animals appeared. Bears lumbered, cattle lowed, squirrels skittered, and rabbits hopped across the dry ground.

But *still*, God wasn't done! God is not only an artist, and not only a storyteller, but also infinitely loving. That love spills like an overflowing cup and graces all the universe. And in His love, God chose to create someone to care for all that He'd made—someone in His own image to reflect His ways as the moon reflects the light of the sun.

And so, God gathered dust from the ground and formed the very first man, whom He named Adam. God breathed life into Adam and then created the first woman, Eve, from Adam's rib, so that together they could be fruitful and have children and care for all the wonders God had made. Then God blessed them both and placed them in a beautiful garden where trees dripped with ripe fruit, and where the tree of life itself—a tree that granted eternal life!—stretched its branches skyward. There, Adam and Eve could flourish as vibrantly as the surrounding plants, with God tenderly watching over them.

With His creation now complete and brimming with life, God rested and gazed upon all He had so marvelously made.

This is the story of our ancestors. It's a story that should have ended here, in the garden with "and they lived happily ever after."

But the story was just beginning.

- God made everything in the universe—yes, everything! Take a moment to look around you and think about His power and magnificence. Thank Him for all He's created!

- Knowing that every person on earth is made in God's image, how should we treat one another?

More of the Story—Read Psalm 139. God created you and has known you since before you were born. How does this fact change your view of God?

Illustrations by Jade van der Zalm

The Curse in the Garden

*Genesis 2–3; Psalm 139; Matthew 10:30;
Romans 1:18–21; 3:23; 5:12; 6:23; Revelation 12:9*

God provided for Adam and Eve's every need in the garden of Eden. They never hurt their backs or broke a sweat for their food, and they never had to harvest it, knead it, pound it, or bake it. Instead, by God's word trees sprang from the soil, heavy with delicious fruit to eat. Best of all, Adam and Eve were with God, the creator of the universe, who loved them.

But Adam and Eve decided all this wasn't enough.

God had only one rule for Adam and Eve. Just *one* rule. He allowed them to eat from any tree in the garden except for the tree of the knowledge of good and evil. From the time they had drawn their first breaths, Adam and Eve had only known the light of God's love; to open their eyes to evil would smear a stain upon their hearts. God warned them never to eat from the tree, or they would die.

After all God had provided for Adam and Eve, following this rule should have been simple for them. But Satan, a disgraced angel cast out of heaven, took the form of a serpent, twisted God's words into lies, and tempted Adam and Eve to disobey.

"No! You will certainly not die," the serpent hissed as he slithered toward Eve. "In fact, God knows that when you eat it your eyes will be opened and you will be like God, knowing good and evil."

Eve looked and looked at the forbidden fruit on the tree. She longed to taste its sweetness. Not only was the fruit lovely to behold and seemed delicious to eat, but according to the serpent it would also make her like God! And so, ignoring God's words, she reached for the fruit, sank her teeth into it, and passed it to Adam.

Surely, Adam would refuse. Surely, as the one whom God had given dominion over the earth, he would follow God's ways.

Oh, no. Adam ate the fruit as well, and as soon as it passed his lips, disaster broke into the world. He looked at Eve, and shame flooded over them both as they realized what they had done. When they heard God approaching, they hid like cowards—as if the Almighty God, who knows even our thoughts, couldn't spy them in any hiding spot.

"Did you eat from the tree that I commanded you not to eat from?" God asked.

What do you think Adam and Eve should have done?

Oh, friend, they didn't apologize. They didn't confess. Their hearts had darkened, and they chose their own way rather than God's.

"The woman You made gave me the fruit!" Adam said.

"The serpent deceived me!" Eve said.

They acted despicably. And with their actions, sin—disobedience against God—burst into the world, spoiling all the loveliness God had created.

From then on, all would be different. A curse would begin to spread over the ground. The soil would dry up and choke with weeds. Childbirth would bring cries of pain.

Worst of all, God expelled Adam and Eve from the garden, never to return, and never to eat from the tree of life.

Sin stained every human heart thereafter. Generation after generation, year after year, hour after hour, people behaved wickedly, and as punishment they returned to the dust. They died, just as God had warned.

This is our story. This is why we don't do what we should. We're born with sin, cut off from God, separated from the One we need more than light and air.

But take heart—the story doesn't end here.

Before He banished Adam and Eve from the garden, God made them clothes to shield them from the cold and the driving rain. Then He promised to send a Savior. Many, many years later, one of Eve's descendants would crush the serpent beneath His heel. He would defeat Satan and reverse the curse, so God's people might again live in His presence—not for a time, but forever.

A Savior was coming! All creation longed for His arrival. When, oh when would He come?

- God clothed Adam and Eve before He sent them out of the garden. What does this reveal about God's character?

- What does God's promise of a Savior tell you about God?

More of the Story—Think of times when you've done something you knew you shouldn't. What does this story teach you about those times? Why don't we do what we should? Hint: read Romans 3:10–12.

To whom can you tell this story today?

Illustrations by Sarah Horne

The Great Flood
Genesis 6–9

After God banished Adam and Eve from the garden, He blessed them with children, who had more children, who had even more children . . . on and on and on, until people multiplied over the face of the earth. And the more people prospered, the more despicably they behaved. In every green valley, thirsty desert, and shady forest, people stole and lied, murdered and hurt one another. Their every thought turned toward evil.

When God saw His people destroying each other, He grieved in His heart. He decided He would cleanse all the world of their wickedness in a great flood. And yet God would not forget His promise to Adam and Eve to send a Savior.

In those days, Noah was the only man who loved God and followed Him. To save Noah and his family,

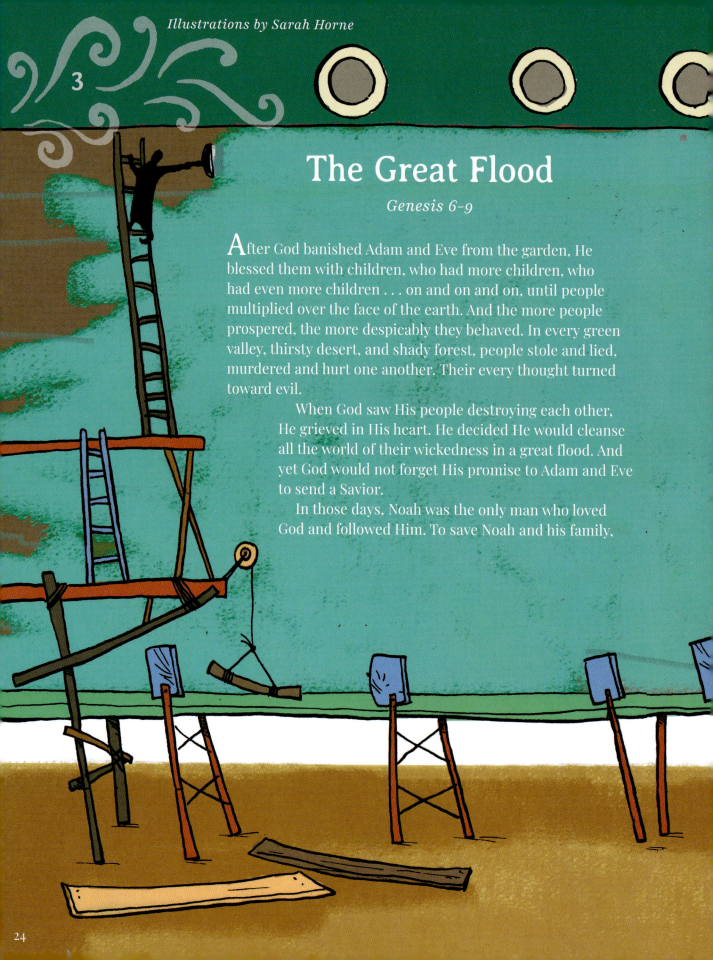

God told Noah to build an enormous ship, called an ark, and to gather two of every kind of animal—everything that crept and crawled and flew and galloped—into the boat. God promised to carry Noah, his family, and the animals safely through the flood, so they all could flourish on the earth after the floodwaters receded.

Noah trusted God and rushed to work—sawing, hammering, and slathering beams in sticky tar. The ark was unlike any boat you've ever seen! It stretched longer than a football field and towered three stories tall. For many long years, Noah pounded and chiseled wood and sanded and wedged more wood until the ark was complete.

Finally, he herded two of every kind of animal into the ark—zebras and caribou, toucans and marmosets, aardvarks, alligators, and great, lumbering elephants. After they crammed squawking and screeching and roaring and baying into the ark, Noah and his family hurried inside. Then God shut the door.

Just as God had promised, the flood came.

CRASH. The windows of heaven opened, and torrents of rain began to pound the earth.

WHOOSH. Water gushed from deep in the earth, spraying skyward and swamping the dry land.

Steadily the waters rose higher and higher, swallowing up the boulders, then the trees, and then even the peaks of the mountains. As the earth disappeared, the ark floated on the water, bobbing like a cork on a stormy sea. Noah and his family huddled together inside and waited for the rain to stop its endless thundering on the roof.

They waited. And waited. And waited.

Finally, after forty long, dreary, seasick days and nights, the rain stopped.

Yet *still* they waited, crouched in their floating zoo as it swayed back and forth and back again.

Would the waters ever drain away? Had God forgotten Noah, after all?

What do you think?

After 150 days, God sent a wind to blow over the waters, and slowly the flood rolled back like a withdrawn curtain. The ark lurched, a crunch sounded, and the ship grounded on mountains that were still under the water.

Yet still, Noah and his family waited! He sent out a dove to search for dry land, but for days the dove brought no sign. Then, finally, it returned with a fresh olive leaf in its beak. The flood had receded!

"Come out, and bring your family with you!" God called. "Be fruitful and multiply on the earth!"

Noah and his family crept out of the ark to discover that all the ground had dried. The sun shone warm and brilliant over the newly washed earth. Trees again shook out clusters of leaves, and plants unfurled toward the sunlight.

As all the animals ran and slithered and swooped out from the ark, God emblazoned a colorful rainbow across the sky. "I have set my bow in the clouds," God said. "Never again shall there be a flood to destroy the earth."

This, dear friend, is the story of God's promise to the earth—and to you. Every time you glimpse a rainbow shimmering in the sky, you can remember the promise God kept to Noah when He carried him safely over the waters.

And you can remember the promise God made to us, to send a Savior so we might live with Him forever.

- What will you think the next time you see a rainbow in the sky?

- God kept His promise to Noah. What does this tell you about God?

More of the Story—Read Hebrews 11:7. Thinking about this verse and what you know about Noah's story, what do you think *faith* means?

Illustrations by Ken Daley

4

The Tower to the Sky

Genesis 10:10; 11:1–9; Revelation 7:9

After the floodwaters receded, God blessed Noah's sons with children, who had more children, who had even more children . . . on, and on, and on. And the more people prospered, the more despicably they behaved.

How could this be, after all God had done? He had stamped a sign of His promise in the sky! Every time a rainbow arced over the horizon, people could look up at it, remember, and rejoice. In those days all people spoke the same language, and so the story of God's love could spread far and wide.

They could tell it while traveling along the way, while gathering fruit and hunting, while sharing the night's fire, over and over and over. Everyone on earth should have whispered God's name with thanksgiving and awe.

But the people didn't think about God's wonders. They didn't remember His promises or His love or the meaning of that rainbow in the clouds. Instead, the seed of sin worked evil in their hearts, and they held tightly to the same twisted, wicked thought that had tempted Adam and Eve in the garden: *We want to be like God.*

In one city, this lust for glory dragged the people into disaster.

After the flood, God had commanded everyone to have families and travel all over the earth, caring for every blade of grass and lowing animal. But some decided they knew better. They gathered together, settled on a plain called Shinar, and built a city. They wanted their city to be the greatest in the world.

First, the people packed clay into molds—*SLOP*—to make bricks. Then they dried these bricks by blazing fires until steam *HISSED* from the clay and the blocks hardened like stone. They stacked the bricks, one after another, and sealed the cracks between them with pitch.

And they decided to build more than just a city.

What else do you think the people built with all these bricks?

Perhaps they built homes to shelter the wandering, to keep them safe from the cold and the driving rain?

Perhaps they built a temple to honor God, who had saved them from the floodwaters?

Oh no, friend. The seed of sin still lurked in their hearts.

"Let's build a tower!" they said. "Let's build a tower so high that its top scrapes the heavens! Then everyone who sees it will know how powerful *we* are."

And so, they stacked bricks, one after the next, after the next, after the next, higher and higher, until the tower reached toward heaven.

Of course, God was watching. He saw the wickedness and selfishness with which the people built, and He grieved in His heart. If they continued, they would drift farther and farther away from Him, farther and farther away from everything good, true, and lovely.

So, God mixed up their words! He broke the single, shared language they had all spoken into dozens of different languages. Suddenly, the people working so furiously to build their glorious tower couldn't understand one another!

Can you imagine seeing and hearing this scene?

The people molding blocks and working the kiln would speak to one another and hear only gibberish. Workers hauling bricks and spreading pitch would gape at each other when their words didn't make sense. Drafted plans, discarded because only one person could read them, would float away on the wind. Imagine the shouting and the angry faces!

With the people's words now muddled, work suddenly stopped. No more bricks were stacked, and the tower slouched unfinished and forgotten. Eventually the people wandered away, scattering to distant corners of the earth. And the abandoned city was thereafter called *Babel*, which in Hebrew means "confusion," because the Lord confused the languages of all who lived there.

And yet, God promises that one day all people will join together and worship Him as one. Every nation will stand together, rejoicing and praising His name with one shared voice.

The story was not over. God was making a way.

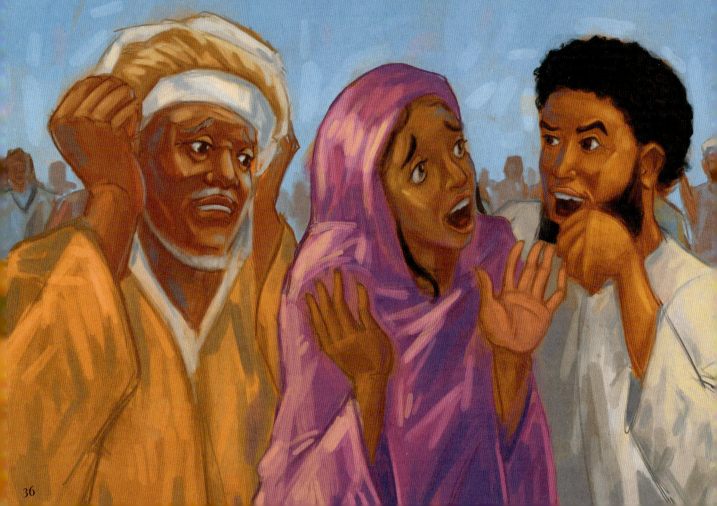

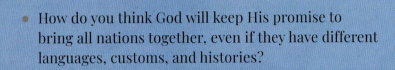

- How do you think God will keep His promise to bring all nations together, even if they have different languages, customs, and histories?

- Working hard is a good thing . . . but not when we do it for the wrong reasons! Can you think of an example today of how people work hard to glorify themselves instead of God?

More of the Story—Read Colossians 3:23–25. How do these verses relate to Babel? How can they guide you?

Illustrations by Breezy Brookshire

5

The Promise in the Stars

Genesis 12:1–9; 13:14–18; 15–17; 21:1–7

After people from Babel scattered all over the earth, they had more children, who had even more children . . . and on, and on, and on.

One of Noah's great-great-bajillion-great grandsons was named Abram. He lived in a land where people worshipped the moon, and although Abram was rich and comfortable, his heart was heavy because his wife, Sarai, couldn't have children of her own. Furthermore, Abram didn't know God.

When Abram was seventy-five years old, the Lord spoke to him for the first time. "Leave your home and go to the land I will show you, and I will make of you a great nation," God said. "In you all the families of the earth shall be blessed."

Imagine: What did Abram think when he heard this message? What expression may he have had on his face?

Go? Go where? And yet, even though he didn't understand, Abram trusted God. He gathered all his silver and his gold, his livestock and his servants, and he and Sarai followed the Lord's command. They left their home and walked and walked and walked across hills and fields and bare, barren rock. They had no idea where God might lead them, but they trusted and followed.

When they reached the land of Canaan, the Lord spoke to Abram again. "All the land that you see I will give to you and to your family forever. I will make your offspring as numerous as the grains of dust on the earth."

Could you count all the grains of dust on earth?

Abram couldn't! *How can I have children and grandchildren and great-grandchildren when I am so old and my wife can't have babies?* he wondered. Yet Abram trusted in God and believed.

Years passed. Abram grew older and older. As the long years piled up and more wrinkles creased his face, no children arrived, and questions crept into Abram's mind. *Had God forgotten His promise?* Abram asked God for guidance, and in response God guided him outside on a clear night. "Look up to heaven and count the stars," God said. Abram raised his eyes skyward, where stars dotted across the dark heavens like silver dust, tens upon hundreds upon thousands, as thick as honey. "So shall your family be," God said.

As many children and grandchildren and great-great-bajillion-great grandchildren as stars in the sky? How could this be? As assurance of His promise, God made a covenant with Abram. He commanded Abram to prepare animals for an offering, and while Abram was sleeping, a smoking pot and a flaming torch appeared and moved through the sacrifice as a seal of God's promise.

More years went by, and more, and more. Still, no baby arrived. Finally, when Abram was ninety-nine years old, God appeared to him and renamed him *Abraham*, which means "father of a multitude." "I will give you a son by your wife," God promised, and He renamed her *Sarah*, which means "princess," because she would give rise to kings of nations.

At these words, Abraham fell on his face and laughed. "Will a child be born to a man who is a hundred years old? Will Sarah, who is ninety years old, have a baby?"

Sarah, too, laughed. "I am old and worn out!" she said.

"Is anything too hard for the LORD?" God said.

What do you think?

Sure enough, the most amazing thing happened! Sarah's womb swelled. Tiny feet kicked her awake at night. At just the right time, Abraham and Sarah's son entered the world.

"God has made laughter for me!" Sarah cried with joy. "Everyone who hears will laugh over me." And they named their baby *Isaac*, which means, "he laughs."

Sarah was right. People would laugh for generations to come, because the Lord had blessed Abraham and Sarah with a child whose own family would create new countries. A child who would give rise to kings.

A child whose great-great-bajillion-great grandson, many, many years later, would crush the head of the serpent forever.

- God blessed Abraham and Sarah with a baby when they were about one hundred years old! What does this tell you about God's power? Is anything too hard for the Lord?

- Count the promises God has made and kept so far in this story. What do these show us about God's character?

More of the Story—Read Romans 4:13, and discuss it with a grown-up. What does Abraham's story teach us about faith?

To whom can you tell this story today?

Illustrations by Cornelius Van Wright

6

The Ram in the Thicket

Genesis 22; Hebrews 11:17–19

Isaac grew from a baby to a toddler to a boy and then to a young man. With each new milestone, Abraham adored his son as his most cherished gift.

Which is why, one terrible day, God's command must have been shocking.

Abraham trusted God enough to leave his home and journey to an unknown land. Yet sin lurked in Abraham's heart, just as it lurks in ours. God chose to test Abraham's faith, once and for all. At the time, the test must have broken Abraham's heart.

"Abraham!" God said one day, when Isaac was a young man. "Take your son, your only son Isaac, whom you love, and go to the land of Moriah, and offer him there as a burnt offering on one of the mountains."

What do you think Abraham thought? How do you think he felt?

Sacrifice Isaac? How could this be? After all God had done, after all He'd promised, how could He now demand Isaac's life?

And yet, Abraham knew that God could do all things and always kept His promises. Somehow, in some way Abraham couldn't understand, God would *still* keep His promise to bless all the world through Isaac. If He so desired, God could even raise Isaac from the dead.

And so, Abraham rose early in the morning, clinging to his trust in God, and began the journey. He chopped wood for a burnt offering, loaded it onto a donkey, and then set off with two servants and Isaac toward the mountain.

They traveled for three days, on and on and on, until Abraham could see the summit of the mountain reaching toward the sky. He and Isaac then went on alone. After heaving the wood onto his son's shoulders to carry, Abraham held the fire and the knife. How heavy the blade must have felt in his own palm!

Isaac noticed they'd brought no animal to sacrifice. "We have the fire and the wood, but where is the lamb for the burnt offering?" he asked.

Can you imagine how the words must have choked Abraham's throat? "God will provide the lamb for a burnt offering, my son," Abraham said. Then they continued the long, heavy climb up the mountain, father and son, together.

Finally, the dreaded hour came. When they reached the mountaintop, Abraham built an altar, piled the wood atop it, and then laid Isaac down. With a hand that must have trembled and a heart pounding with anguish, Abraham reached for the knife.

Suddenly, a voice cried out from heaven! "Abraham! Abraham!" God said. "Do not lay your hand on the boy or do anything to him, for now I know that you fear God, seeing you have not withheld your son, your only son, from Me." At the sound of God's voice, Abraham lifted his eyes, and through a sheen of tears he saw a ram caught by his horns in the thicket.

God had provided the sacrifice!

"In your offspring all the nations of the earth will be blessed, because you have obeyed my voice," the Lord told Abraham.

How would you have responded if you were Abraham?

What joy must have washed over him! Can you imagine him pulling his dear son to his chest and weeping into his hair? Can you see him praising God for His faithfulness?

God provided for Abraham and Isaac on the mountaintop. And many, many, many years later, He would provide *for us*.

God didn't take Abraham's only son. But one day He would give *His* only Son so that we might live forever.

- Abraham named the place where this story happened, "The LORD will provide," so others might remember how God provides for us. What can you think about in your life to remind yourself that God provides?

- Just like Abraham, sometimes we don't understand why things happen to us. What does this story teach us about trusting God in difficult times?

More of the Story—This story foreshadows how God would save us from our sins. Read Romans 8:32 and discuss this verse with a grown-up.

Illustrations by Carlos Vélez Aguilera

7

A Brother Betrayed

Genesis 37; 39; 41–47; 50:20; Matthew 26:14–16

Isaac grew up and had children, who had more children, on and on and on. Isaac's son Jacob had a wrestling match with God (**guess who won?**), and so God renamed him *Israel*, meaning "wrestles with God." Israel went on to have twelve sons, each of whom would give rise to an entire tribe of people!

Of all his children, Israel loved his second youngest, Joseph, the most. Israel draped a splendid, multicolored coat around Joseph's shoulders to signal that *Joseph*—rather than the oldest son—was the future head of the family. As the other brothers watched, their faces darkened, and they grumbled with jealousy.

Then Joseph dreamed that one day his own family would bow down to him. When his brothers heard this, their grumblings turned to seething anger! Who was Joseph to rule over *them*?

Their hearts hardened with hatred, until finally one day the brothers attacked Joseph while he tended their father's sheep. "We'll see what will become of his dreams!" they growled.

The brothers stripped Joseph of the coat that had stirred up so much bitterness, hurled him into a pit in the ground, and then sold him to a group of traveling slave traders for twenty pieces of silver. They dipped Joseph's special coat in goat's blood and pretended that a wild animal had eaten him.

Bound in ropes, Joseph trudged through the dust for miles and miles, all the way to Egypt. Would he ever embrace his beloved father again? Would he ever again see his homeland?

Oh yes, friend. God provided for Joseph.

Joseph saw both blessings and hardships in Egypt, both freedom and imprisonment, but all the while God protected him. The pharaoh of Egypt had troubling dreams about seven skinny cows gobbling up seven fat ones, and seven withered ears of corn eating up seven plump ones. The dreams so tormented Pharaoh that he sought help from anyone in the land who could interpret them. The king's advisors tried and failed, over and over; no one could understand the dreams.

No one, that is, except Joseph.

Joseph warned Pharaoh that the dreams threatened seven years of famine, and he advised Pharaoh to store up food in every grain house in his kingdom to prepare. Joseph so impressed Pharaoh that the king made him a leader in the kingdom and put him in charge of storing food!

Just as Joseph had predicted, famine struck. The soil turned parched and dusty. Crops shriveled up. Livestock sickened and died, and hunger nagged every stomach in the land—except in Egypt, where Joseph had stockpiled grain.

Back in Canaan, every member of Israel's family was starving. The very same brothers who'd betrayed Joseph traveled for miles and miles in search of help, and finally they arrived weary and famished at the Egyptian court—where none other than Joseph greeted them.

The brothers didn't recognize Joseph, who now dressed in the fancy clothes of Egyptian royalty. But Joseph recognized them!

How do you think Joseph reacted? Did he yell? Did he scream? Did he give his brothers the punishment they deserved?

Amazingly, Joseph didn't do any of these things. Instead, he *forgave* them, because he saw God at work despite their terrible deeds. "You intended to harm me," he said, "but God intended it for good, to save many lives."

And in keeping with God's promise, Abraham's descendants were kept alive. All of Israel's family—about seventy people!—left Canaan and settled in Egypt. When Joseph and Israel reunited at long last, they fell into each other's arms and wept tears of joy. The whole family thrived under Joseph's care and had children, who had more children, and on and on and on. God kept His promise to make Abraham a father of nations, even when betrayal and famine threatened to destroy Abraham's family forever.

Millennia later, another man, like Joseph, would save God's people even as He suffered. He too would endure betrayal. His life, too, would be cast away for a slave's price of silver.

He too would grant forgiveness.

- Do you ever struggle with jealousy as Joseph's brothers did? We all do sometimes! Pray and ask the Lord to soften your heart toward others.

- Joseph's brothers didn't deserve forgiveness, but he granted it to them. How does this mirror God's treatment of us?

More of the Story—Israel's family would have died in Canaan if Joseph hadn't been sold as a slave in Egypt. What does this teach you about how God works through the hardships in our lives? Read Romans 8:28.

To whom can you tell this story today?

Illustrations by Natalie Peterson

8

The Fire in the Bush

Exodus 1-3; John 8:34-36; Hebrews 11:24-26

After Israel's family settled in Egypt, they spread throughout the land and had children, who had more children, who had even more children . . . and on, and on, and on. And once again, sin threatened to destroy God's people.

After Joseph and his brothers died, a new pharaoh rose to power. He didn't remember how Joseph had saved Egypt from starvation. On the contrary, he saw how numerous the Israelites were in Egypt, and he didn't like it. Not one bit. "There are so many!" Pharaoh said. "What if war breaks out, and the Israelites join our enemies and fight against us?"

To keep them under control, Pharaoh ruthlessly made God's people his slaves. He forced them to work the fields beneath the blistering sun, heave bricks, and slather mortar, all while brutal taskmasters watched their every move. He even commanded the midwives, who helped with childbirth, to drown all baby Israelite boys in the Nile!

How could this happen? Had God forgotten His promise to Abraham? Did He forget to send His Savior?

Oh no, dear friend. God heard His people's cries. He heard, and He would raise up a leader to guide His people to freedom.

During this dreadful time, an Israelite woman gave birth to a son. She hid the boy from the Egyptians for as long as she could, until finally, when he was too big to hide, she placed him in a basket and floated it among the reeds by the riverbank. She prayed that God would guard her dear son.

Imagine the basket bobbing on the water. What would happen to the baby?

How the mother's heart must have torn away and floated along with it! What she didn't know is that the basket she released so tenderly on the river held the hope for her entire nation.

As the basket nestled in the reeds, who should pass by but Pharaoh's daughter! She heard the baby crying, took pity on him, and adopted him as her own child. She named him Moses, which means "to draw out," because she'd drawn him out of the water. And so, just as God had carried Noah safely through the flood, He also saved Moses on the river.

Although Moses lived in the palace, as he grew older the slavery of his people troubled him. It bothered him so much that one day he lashed out and killed an Egyptian he caught mistreating an Israelite. When Pharaoh discovered Moses's crime, he threatened to kill him, and so Moses fled. He settled in a distant land, married, and fell into a new life as a shepherd, far from Egypt and out of earshot of the cries of his people.

But God heard His people's cries. And He had a plan to save them—a plan that involved Moses.

One day, forty years after he'd fled from Egypt, Moses was tending a flock of sheep in the wilderness when he saw an amazing sight. There in front of him, a bush blazed with fire, but the flames neither blackened the branches nor scorched the leaves. The fire licked the sky, but the bush itself did not burn up! To his astonishment, a great voice thundered from within the fire. "Moses! Moses!" the voice said.

It was the voice of God! He promised to deliver His people from slavery and lead them to the land He had promised to Abraham—to Canaan, a land flowing with milk and honey. God commanded Moses to return to Egypt and to demand that Pharaoh set the Israelites free.

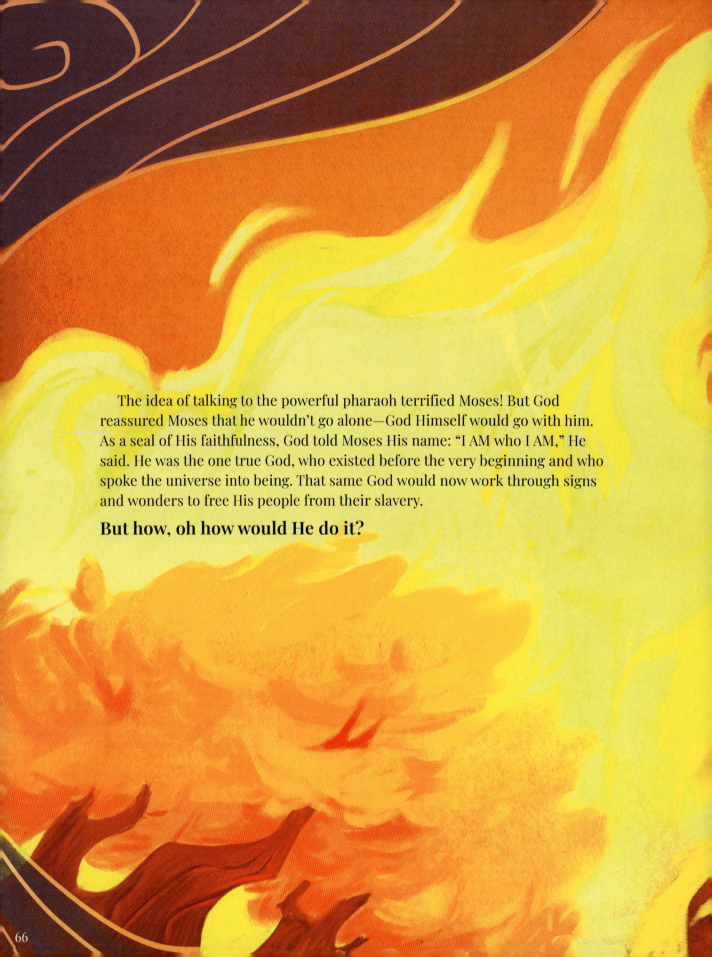

The idea of talking to the powerful pharaoh terrified Moses! But God reassured Moses that he wouldn't go alone—God Himself would go with him. As a seal of His faithfulness, God told Moses His name: "I AM who I AM," He said. He was the one true God, who existed before the very beginning and who spoke the universe into being. That same God would now work through signs and wonders to free His people from their slavery.

But how, oh how would He do it?

- Some people think the Bible is a book of role models and good people. Yet even Moses, who would lead his people to freedom, killed a man! What does this tell you about sin?

- The word for *basket* used in this story is actually the same word for *ark*. How does the story of Moses on the Nile remind you of Noah?

More of the Story—The idea of speaking to Pharaoh frightened Moses. How did God reassure him? Read Isaiah 41:10 and Jeremiah 42:11. How should these verses reassure us?

Illustrations by Thanos Tsilis

9

Storms, Swarms, and Deep, Deep Darkness

Exodus 4-10

The God of Israel says, 'Let my people go!'"

"I will not let Israel go!" said Pharaoh, aghast as Moses and his brother, Aaron, stood before him. "In fact, I'll make their burdens even worse! How dare they challenge the king of Egypt!" As punishment, Pharaoh doubled the Israelites' work and commanded the taskmasters to beat anyone who failed in their duties.

The people cried out for mercy. God had promised to deliver them, but instead things were worse!

What do you think God was doing? Had He abandoned His people?

Oh no, friend. God's magnificent plan had just begun.

"Now you shall see what I will do!" God said. He told Moses that He would perform signs and wonders so everyone would know that *He* was the one true God. You see, the Egyptians bowed down to the sun, to the Nile, and even to frogs that hopped and crocodiles that slithered into the river. God would show His people that He ruled over all these created things, so they would trust in *Him* instead of false gods. Then God would stretch out His hand against Egypt and free His people.

On God's instructions, Moses returned to Pharaoh and again demanded he let the people go.

What do you think Pharaoh said?

"No, I won't!" said Pharaoh.

So God performed His first wonder. Under His command, Moses struck the Nile with his staff, and the river turned to blood! The fish died, the river stank, and the blood poisoned the water. The Egyptians cried out in thirst.

But still, Pharaoh would not let the people go. God had hardened Pharaoh's heart so that all might see the signs and wonders and place their trust in God.

God brought the second plague. Upon His command, Aaron stretched out his hand, and suddenly with a great *CROAK* and *RIBBET* and *BURP*, thousands of frogs swarmed over the land. They invaded people's houses and wriggled into their beds. They crammed into ovens and jammed into serving bowls.

But still, Pharaoh would not let the people go.

So God brought the third plague. Suddenly, gnats coated every inch of ground. They flitted in men's faces, itched women's bare feet, and burrowed into the hides of the livestock.

But still, Pharaoh would not let the people go.

So God brought the fourth plague. Great swarms of flies buzzed and teemed in the Egyptians' homes.

But still, Pharaoh would not let the people go.

So God brought the fifth plague. A disease struck Pharaoh's horses, donkeys, camels, herds, and flocks. All the Egyptians' livestock died.

But still, Pharaoh would not let the people go!

So God brought the sixth plague. Boils swelled and festered on all the Egyptians' skin. Even their animals suffered from sores.

But still, Pharaoh would not let the people go!

So God brought the seventh plague. A hailstorm pounded down from the sky. Thunder crashed, lightning flashed, and bullets of ice pummeled the earth, flattening stalks of grain and shearing branches from every tree.
But *still*, Pharaoh would not let the people go!

So God brought the eighth plague. A wind buffeted the earth and brought with it a swarm of locusts, so many that they clogged the sky and blackened the land. They gobbled up all the plants and the fruit the Egyptians had left.
But *still*, Pharaoh would not let the people go!

So, God brought the ninth plague. He commanded Moses to stretch out his hand toward heaven, and suddenly all of Egypt pitched into darkness. For three days, no glimmer of sunlight warmed the fields or byways of Egypt.

God had protected His people from each plague, but the Egyptians groaned in misery. They pleaded with Pharaoh for help!

But his heart was hardened. *Still*, Pharaoh would not let the people go.

And so, God brought the tenth plague, the most terrible of all.

Would His people finally be delivered from slavery?

- How do these nine plagues demonstrate that God is the one, true God?

- Think back to God's promise to Abraham. How is He keeping faithful to that promise in this story?

More of the Story—Read Romans 1:19–23. How did the Egyptians fulfill what Paul writes about in this passage? Do we act this way too?

Illustrations by Jade van der Zalm

10

A Sea Divided

Exodus 4:22; 11–14; John 1:29; 1 Corinthians 5:7

Even though God warned the Egyptians with frogs, locusts, boils, hail, and deep, dreadful darkness, Pharaoh would *still* not let the Israelites go.

So God brought the most terrible plague of all.

"Israel is my firstborn son," God said. "Because Pharaoh will not let Israel go, this very night all the firstborn sons in Egypt will die, from the firstborn of Pharaoh who sits on the throne to the firstborn of the slave girl at the hand mill."

Then God told His people to get ready. That very night, He would guide them to freedom.

First God would protect His people from the death that would strike Egypt that night. He told each household to sacrifice a lamb in their firstborn's place and to paint their doors with its blood as a sign. When death swept through Egypt, it would pass over the houses marked with the lamb's blood.

Then God commanded each household to roast the lamb and have a quick meal, ready all the while to flee Egypt. There wouldn't be enough time for bread to rise, so they were to eat flat bread instead. They would eat in haste, with their sandals on their feet, their walking sticks in hand, and their belts already tied. To remember what He'd done for them—and what He would *still* do—God told the people to have this meal every year thereafter. God would save Israel from slavery to Egypt through the blood of a lamb; one day, He would save all of us from slavery to sin through the blood of a greater lamb— His own firstborn Son.

The people did as God instructed. When night fell, a terrible wailing echoed over the kingdom. Death had descended over Egypt, and cries of grief rang out as all the Egyptians' firstborn sons died—including Pharaoh's.

"Go!" Pharaoh finally yelled in anguish. "Go and bless me also!" Finally, at long last, God's power had humbled Pharaoh.

But that humility wouldn't last.

All in a hurry, God's people fled Egypt. God provided for them even as they ran, working in the hearts of the Egyptians to give them belongings along the way. They all marched from the cities in which they had moaned and toiled, and they strode eastward, toward the land God had promised them. And God Himself guided them as they went! He appeared before the crowd in a pillar of smoke by day and a pillar of fire that lit up the night. He remained with them every hour and never departed.

Imagine this scene! What would it be like to walk with God beside you?

They walked and walked until they reached the huge, heaving expanse of the Red Sea. There, suddenly, their shouts of joy turned to screams of panic. The firelight of torches flickered behind them and glinted off the upraised swords of Pharaoh's army. He'd chased after them! There God's people stood, with the Red Sea billowing before them and Pharaoh's army thundering in pursuit behind.

How, oh how could they escape?

Upon God's command, Moses raised his staff. Suddenly, with a great roaring wind, the Red Sea split in two! Great walls of water surged skyward, revealing a path of dry land to lead the Israelites to safety.

Moses cried out, and the people ran across the path.

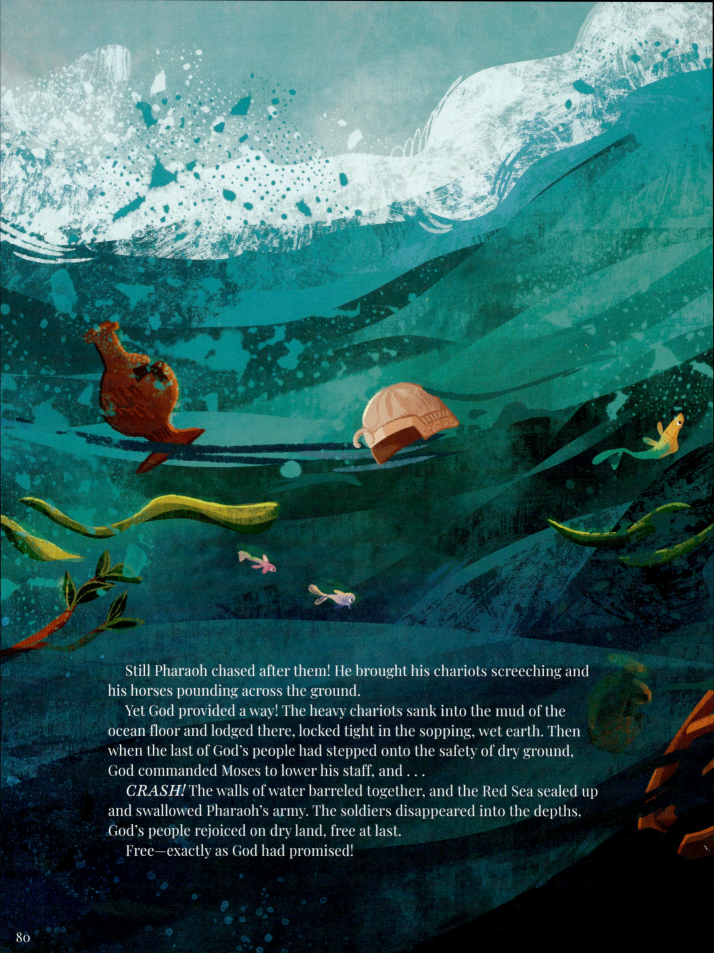

Still Pharaoh chased after them! He brought his chariots screeching and his horses pounding across the ground.

Yet God provided a way! The heavy chariots sank into the mud of the ocean floor and lodged there, locked tight in the sopping, wet earth. Then when the last of God's people had stepped onto the safety of dry ground, God commanded Moses to lower his staff, and . . .

CRASH! The walls of water barreled together, and the Red Sea sealed up and swallowed Pharaoh's army. The soldiers disappeared into the depths. God's people rejoiced on dry land, free at last.

Free—exactly as God had promised!

- The Passover foreshadows the Savior who would come to rescue us from our sins. What kind of Savior would this be?

- Did the Israelites do anything to save themselves from slavery?

More of the Story—Read John 8:34, and now think about the last question. Israel needed God to save them from slavery. Whom do we need to save us from slavery to sin?

To whom can you tell this story today?

Illustrations by Kristi Smith

11

The Wilderness

Exodus 15–17; 19–20; 32; Numbers 11; 13–14; 20:2–13; Deuteronomy 8:7–10

CRASH! The waves swept together, the army disappeared, and in the next instant the Red Sea sealed up again. After generations of misery and heartbreak, the Israelites breathed the air as free people. God had done it!

"Sing to the Lord, for he has triumphed gloriously!" the people sang.

But their jubilation didn't last. To reach the Promised Land, they had to cross a vast, barren wilderness. Dust billowed up—*POOF!*—from beneath their sandals as they trudged. As the sun glared and sweat drenched their brows, their memory of God's triumph fizzled away, and the Israelites behaved despicably.

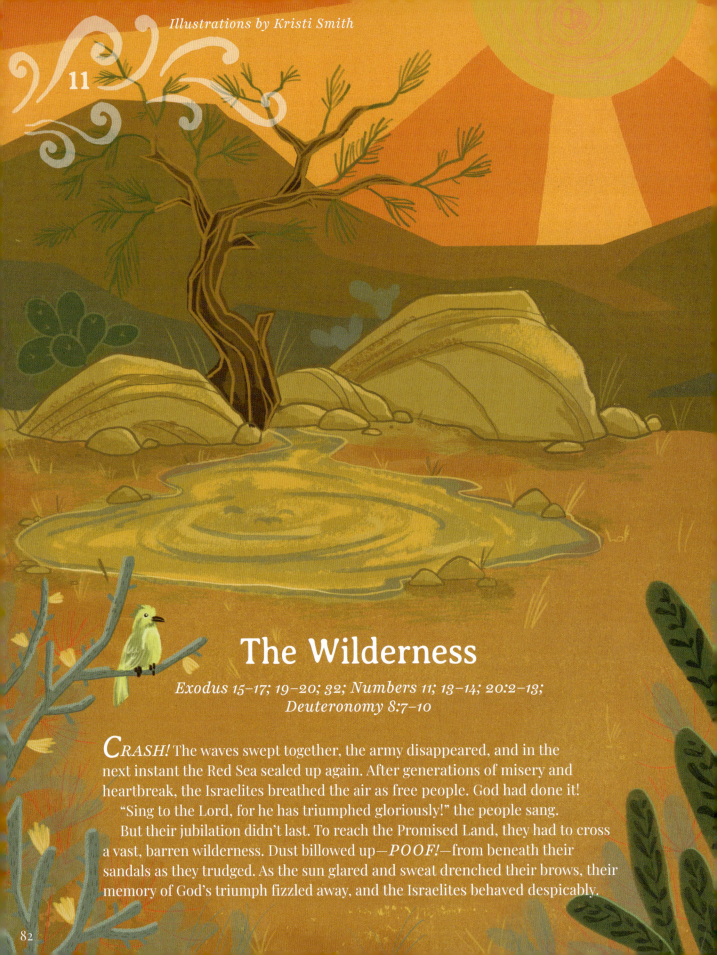

First, they grumbled for water. After they trudged and trudged over the bone-dry earth until their tongues stuck to the roofs of their mouths, they discovered a spring . . . but it tasted bitter. "What shall we drink?" the people whined.

God provided. Moses threw a log into the spring, and the water turned cool and sweet.

Then the people grumbled for food. "You've brought us into this wilderness to starve us to death!" they cried.

Again, God provided. Every morning He dusted the ground with a white, sugary food called manna for His people to gather, as much as they could eat. And every evening, he filled the skies with quail to fill their bellies.

Then the people grumbled for water *again*. "Why did you bring us out of Egypt, to kill us and our children and our livestock with thirst?" they cried.

Again, God provided! He told Moses to strike a rock, and a fountain of water gushed out. And even as the people grumbled, God still led them as a pillar of smoke by day and a pillar of fire by night, on and on, guiding them with each step.

Finally, God brought the Israelites to a towering mountain where He appeared at the very top in a great cloud that roared with thunder and sizzled with lightning. There He gave them rules to ensure they would love Him, love each other, and thrive. "We'll obey!" the people cried out.

But then they committed the worst grumbling of all.

God called Moses up the mountainside. In his presence God etched the most important rules, called the Ten Commandments, onto stone tablets so the people would always remember. While Moses was away, however, the Israelites grew impatient. They demanded that Aaron make them new gods to lead them across the wilderness.

What would you have said to the grumbling people?

Unbelievably, Aaron said yes.

Forgetting all God had done, Aaron collected gold jewelry, melted it down, and then molded it into the shape of a calf. Then, while their true God still hovered on the mountain, the Israelite people bowed down to worship this lifeless statue as their god!

Still, God provided. He punished many that day for their idolatry, but in His mercy rather than abandon them He led them onward. Finally, after many months of guiding His people through the wilderness and filling their bellies daily, God brought them to the edge of Canaan. The land was as lush as He'd promised, with fertile soil and trees heavy with ripe pomegranates and figs. Fountains and springs bubbled from the ground and flowed out to water the valleys and hills. Wheat and barley swayed in the fields. A single cluster of grapes was so enormous that two men had to carry it on a staff between them!

Surely, the people wouldn't grumble now, after all God had done? What do you think?

Oh, dear friend, the seed of sin still lurked in their hearts, and they behaved despicably.

God told the people to march into Canaan and claim it as their own, but when scouts glimpsed the tall and strong men already living there, the Israelites forgot God's promises and cowered in fear. "They're stronger than us!" the people sniveled. "We can't go into Canaan! Giants live there!"

Enough was enough. God declared that none of the people He'd rescued from Egypt would set foot on the rich soil of the Promised Land. Not even Moses could enter, as he, too, had disobeyed God in a moment of anger! Although God would still give the land to their children, all the people who grumbled against Him would live the rest of their days in the wilderness.

And so, the Israelites wandered and wandered for forty years in the dust.

But God would keep His promise. The day for Israel to return home would finally come.

- The Israelites praised God after He saved them, but they immediately grumbled when hunger and thirst struck. It's easy to thank God when things are going well! How can we be sure to still thank Him when we're unhappy?

- The Israelites had seen God perform the most amazing wonders in Egypt, but they still worshipped a golden calf. What does this teach us about sin?

More of the Story—Read Psalm 77:9–15. How can you remember God's love even when things aren't going well?

To whom can you tell this story today?

Illustrations by Jesus Lopez

The Trumpets and the Tumbling Wall

Deuteronomy 8:2–4; 18:15; 34:1–8; Joshua 1:1–9; 3; 6; Hebrews 3:1–6

For forty years, the Israelites wandered in the wilderness. And yet, even over all those long years, God cared for them. As they walked and trudged and marched, their feet never swelled. As the sun beat down and wind lashed them, their clothes never frayed. Every morning manna blanketed the earth like snow, and every evening quail fluttered in the skies.

Finally, Moses's years on earth ended. Before he died, he reminded the people of all God had done for them, and he urged them not to forget. Moses told them to look for a prophet like him—a prophet *greater* than him—called the Messiah, or the Christ. He would be the Savior whom God would send.

Moses climbed a mountaintop, and God showed him the land into which He would lead the people—a land green and sprawling, stretching all the way to the glittering sea. After Moses saw the fruits of God's promises, he drew his last breath.

Tears stained the people's cheeks as they mourned the passing of their beloved prophet, the one who met with God face-to-face. And yet, like a new plant rising through the soil after a forest fire, God raised up a new leader for Israel: Joshua. Joshua had been faithful in the wilderness, and so God called him to guide His people into the Promised Land. The journey would be long and hard. The road ahead would include battles with people mightier than the Israelites, people who sheltered behind sturdy fortresses. And yet God promised Joshua that he would succeed. "Be strong and courageous," God told Joshua. "Do not be frightened, and do not be dismayed, for the LORD your God is with you wherever you go."

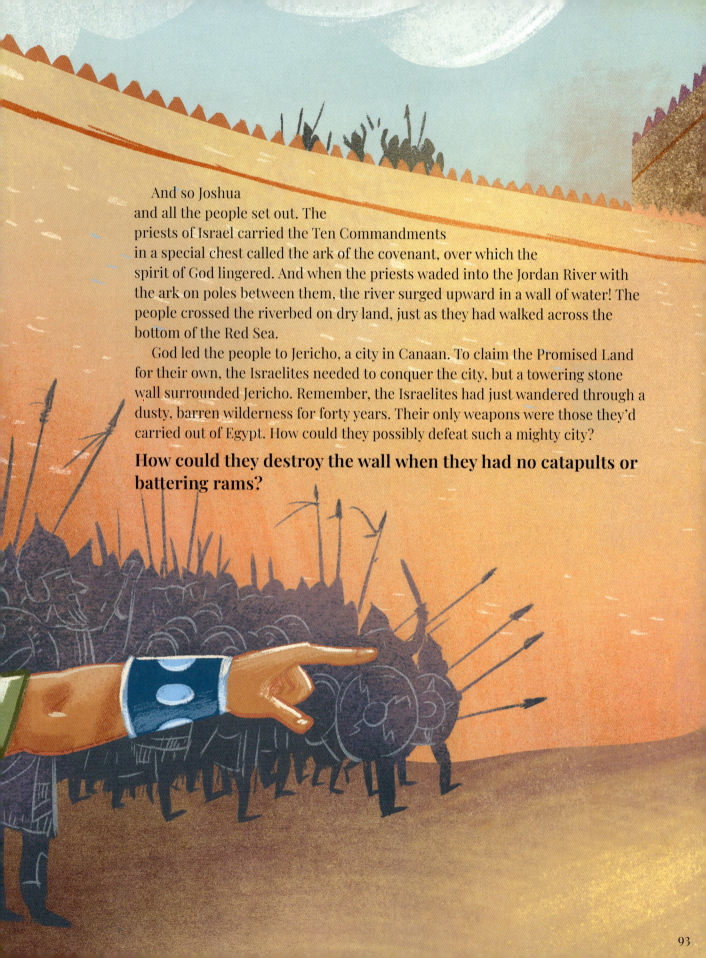

And so Joshua and all the people set out. The priests of Israel carried the Ten Commandments in a special chest called the ark of the covenant, over which the spirit of God lingered. And when the priests waded into the Jordan River with the ark on poles between them, the river surged upward in a wall of water! The people crossed the riverbed on dry land, just as they had walked across the bottom of the Red Sea.

God led the people to Jericho, a city in Canaan. To claim the Promised Land for their own, the Israelites needed to conquer the city, but a towering stone wall surrounded Jericho. Remember, the Israelites had just wandered through a dusty, barren wilderness for forty years. Their only weapons were those they'd carried out of Egypt. How could they possibly defeat such a mighty city?

How could they destroy the wall when they had no catapults or battering rams?

93

With God leading them, to bring down the wall all the people needed to do was walk.

God told the Israelites to march around Jericho once a day for six days. On each of those days, seven priests carrying the ark of the covenant were to blast continually on rams' horn trumpets. The people, however, were to march in silence.

Then, on the seventh day, the crowd would march seven times around the city, and the priests would blast their trumpets for a long, loud note. "When you hear the sound of the trumpet," God said, "then all the people shall shout with a great shout, and the wall of the city will fall down flat."

And so Joshua rallied the people. On the first day, they encircled the city, blasting their trumpets—*TOO-TOO-TOOM!*

They did the same on the second day, and the third, and the fourth, the fifth, and the sixth—*TOO-TOO-TOOM!*

Finally, the seventh day arrived. The people rose when the first blush of sunrise stained the sky. They marched around the city seven times, and the priests blew their trumpets. Then Joshua cried out, "Shout, for the LORD has given you the city!"

As the trumpet blast died, the crowd roared! Then a great rumbling shook the earth, and . . . *CRASH!* The mighty wall of Jericho collapsed into a pile of rubble! As the bricks toppled down and a cloud of dust covered the sky, the Israelites rushed into the city and claimed it.

God had delivered Canaan into their hands—just as He'd promised!

- Even though the people in the wilderness had disobeyed God, He brought their children into the Promised Land. What does this reveal about God's character?

- Count the promises God has kept. What do you think about God's promise to send a Savior?

More of the Story—Did the people bring down the walls of Jericho on their own? Read Hebrews 11:30. What should we remember when we try to do hard things in our own lives?

Illustrations by Carlos Vélez Aguilera

13

The Shepherd King

1 Samuel 8; 9:2; 10:17–19, 24; 13:12–14; 16:1–13; 17:1–49

At long last, Canaan belonged to the Israelites, just as God had promised! Surely the people would honor Him now.

What do you think?

Oh, no. The seed of sin still lurked in their hearts. They wanted to go their own way, rather than God's, just like Adam and Eve, the people in Noah's time, the people at Babel, and even the Israelites in the wilderness.

"We want a king like all the other nations have!" they whined. This complaint was ridiculous. They already had the very best king of all—God!

But they insisted, and so God gave them over to their own stubbornness. For their king, He chose Saul, the tallest and handsomest man in Israel. Saul certainly *looked* kingly! And yet his impressive looks hid a heart that didn't love God. When Saul repeatedly broke God's commandments, God chose a new king. A better king. And the last king anyone would have expected.

God told His prophet, Samuel, to find the new king in the house of Jesse, a shepherd living in the town of Bethlehem. When Samuel arrived, Jesse's eldest son stepped forward. He was tall and strong. Surely this would be God's chosen king!

God said, "No."

The next oldest son appeared. Would he be the one?

Nope! God said no over and over until seven sons had come and gone. Only one remained: David, the youngest, who was still in the fields tending the sheep.

"This is he!" God said when David appeared. Although he wasn't nearly as strong, tall, or fearsome as Saul, David was a man after God's own heart—as the rest of Israel would soon see.

Shortly afterward, Israel's enemies gathered a great army on a mountaintop. Every morning, a warrior named Goliath, who towered nine feet tall, lumbered forward, a javelin strapped to his shoulders and his bronze armor flashing. "Send a man to fight me!" he would bellow. Rather than fight, all the Israelites cowered behind one another in terror.

All except one.

Young David was bringing grain and cheese to his brothers in the army when he heard Goliath's taunts. "Who is this man, that he should defy the armies of the living God?" David asked in outrage. With determination pulsing in his heart, he approached Saul and volunteered to fight Goliath.

"But you're just a boy!" Saul said.

"I've killed lions and bears while watching my father's sheep," David said. "The LORD who delivered me from the paw of the lion and the paw of the bear will deliver me from Goliath."

And so Saul clothed David in armor and strapped a sword to his back. But David was so young and small that the armor didn't fit! He took it off and decided that his only weapons would be his sling, his shepherd's staff, five smooth stones . . . and his trust in the almighty God.

Goliath scoffed at the sight of the tiny shepherd boy venturing onto the grass. "Am I a dog, that you come to me with sticks?" Goliath roared.

"You come to me with a sword and a spear and a javelin," David shouted back, "but I come to you in the name of the LORD! The battle is the LORD's, and he will give you into our hand."

Goliath gnashed his teeth, growled with rage, and charged across the battlefield toward David!

David rushed to meet him. He reached into his bag for one of the stones.

Goliath barreled onward, most likely frothing like a frenzied bull. Closer and closer he drew, his hot breath misting into clouds.

David tucked the stone into his sling and swung it above his head.

Goliath roared and raised his sword high! Just a few steps, and he'd be upon David, his blade swiping through the air . . .

WHOOSH! CRACK! At just the right moment, David's sling sailed through the air, and the stone struck Goliath on the forehead!

With a last, long gasp, the giant fell onto the ground face-first and lay still . . . never to rise again. God's chosen king stood triumphant on the battlefield, armed with a sling, a stone . . . and his trust in God!

- What do you think God meant when He said that David was a man after His own heart?

- Although Saul looked impressive, he wasn't a good king. What does this teach us about what's important to God?

More of the Story—Read Psalm 23. David wrote this prayer! What does it tell you about God, and about David's relationship with Him?

To whom can you tell this story today?

Illustrations by Matt Forsyth

14

The Cries of the Prophets

1 Kings 18:20–40; 2 Kings 25:8–21; 2 Chronicles 36:15–21; Psalm 22; Isaiah 34:4–5; 53:3–6; 61:1–2; Jeremiah 1:13–16; 23:5; 29:10; Lamentations 3:21–23; Daniel 7:13–14; Hosea 9:3; Joel 2:32; Zechariah 9:9; Micah 5:2

David's time as king was like a burst of light in the darkness, when for a brief moment His love for God flashed brightly in Israel. Too quickly, however, that glow faded away. Sin lurked in David's heart, and he behaved wickedly, as had all the people before him . . . and after him.

Years after David died, the nation of Israel fractured into two kingdoms—the northern kingdom of Israel and the southern kingdom of Judah. A long line of wicked kings led God's people farther and farther from His ways. In every green valley, dry desert, and shady forest, people stole and lied, murdered and hurt one another. Their every thought turned toward evil.

When God saw all this wickedness, His heart was grieved, and so He sent prophets to warn the people to repent.

One prophet, Elijah, challenged the priests of a false god named Baal to a contest: they would all offer a sacrifice, but only the one, true God would send down flames to burn up the offering. Upon Elijah's urging, 450 priests sacrificed a bull to Baal. For hours they cried out, "O Baal, answer us!" But no fire streaked down from the sky, and no voice broke the silence.

Then it was Elijah's turn. The moment he called out to God, fire blazed down—*WHOOSH!*—and consumed not only the offering but also the wood and the stones and the dust. It even licked up the water in the trench around the altar! The people who saw fell on their faces and cried, "The LORD, He is God!"

But they soon forgot. Still, the people went on sinning.

More prophets warned the people. Hosea predicted that Assyria and Egypt would conquer Israel. After a plague of locusts struck the land, Joel warned the people to call on the name of the Lord to be saved.

But the people didn't listen. Still, they went on sinning.

The prophet Jeremiah saw a vision of a boiling pot in the north, a warning that destruction was coming.

But the people didn't listen. Still, they went on sinning!

And so, finally, punishment came. A fierce army from the northern kingdom of Babylon swept over the capital city of Jerusalem in a wave of terror. Fire raged through the streets. Soldiers looted homes and plundered the marketplace. Even the marvelous temple of God crumbled to the ground. The soldiers bound any survivors in chains and dragged them away as captives.

Afterward, Jeremiah wandered the streets of Jerusalem and wailed. Had the Lord forgotten His people? Had He forgotten His promise to Abraham?

What would you have thought if you were with Jeremiah? How could you have comforted him?

Then among the rubble and the ruins, Jeremiah remembered who God was, and he had hope: "The steadfast love of the LORD never ceases," he said. "His mercies never come to an end; they are new every morning; great is your faithfulness."

Jeremiah knew that after seventy years, God would return the exiles to Jerusalem. And best of all, he and the prophets glimpsed the Savior whom God would one day send to stamp out the seed of sin in our hearts.

Jeremiah foretold that the Savior would arise from the line of King David. Micah prophesied He would come from the humble town of Bethlehem. Zechariah declared He would ride on the colt of a donkey.
Daniel, whom God saved from the lions' den, called Him the Son of Man and said He would arrive on the clouds and have everlasting rule over the world.

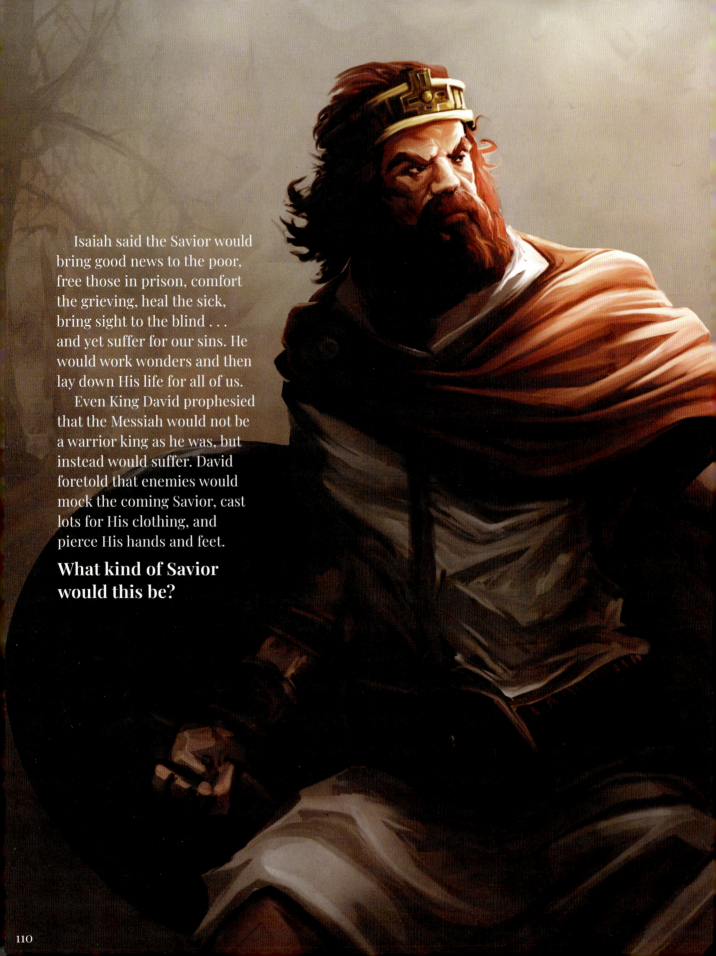

Isaiah said the Savior would bring good news to the poor, free those in prison, comfort the grieving, heal the sick, bring sight to the blind . . . and yet suffer for our sins. He would work wonders and then lay down His life for all of us.

Even King David prophesied that the Messiah would not be a warrior king as he was, but instead would suffer. David foretold that enemies would mock the coming Savior, cast lots for His clothing, and pierce His hands and feet.

What kind of Savior would this be?

- Even though the prophets sent warning after warning, the people didn't repent. How does this remind you of the Israelites' time in the wilderness?

More of the Story—Read Psalm 14:2–3. Can any of us get rid of sin on our own?

Read Isaiah 53 with a grown-up. What did Isaiah say about the Savior whom God would send?

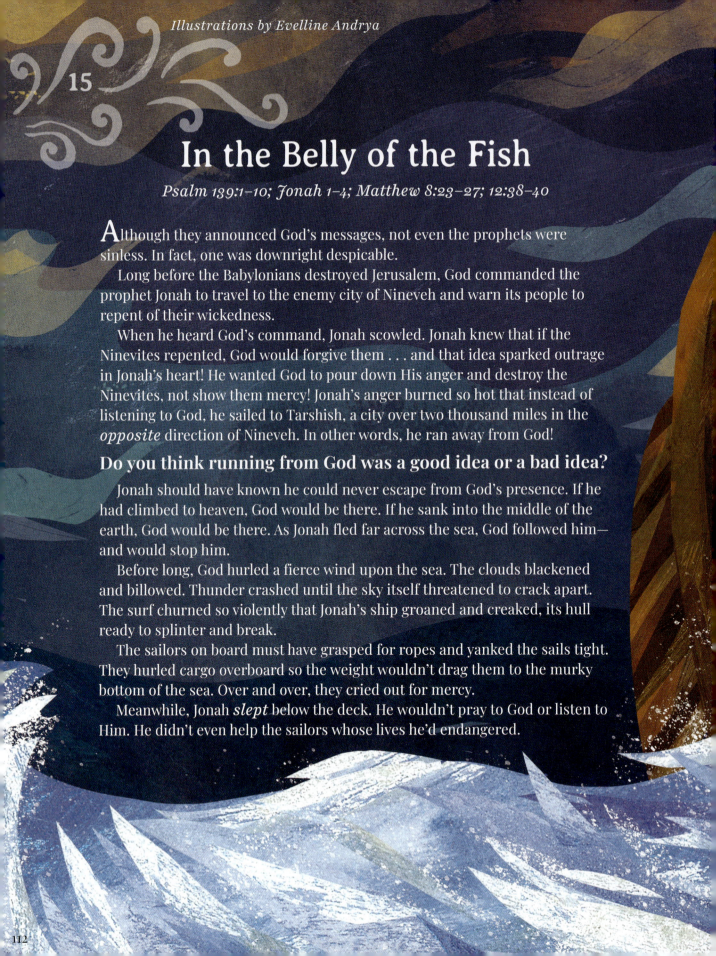

Illustrations by Evelline Andrya

15

In the Belly of the Fish

Psalm 139:1–10; Jonah 1–4; Matthew 8:23–27; 12:38–40

Although they announced God's messages, not even the prophets were sinless. In fact, one was downright despicable.

Long before the Babylonians destroyed Jerusalem, God commanded the prophet Jonah to travel to the enemy city of Nineveh and warn its people to repent of their wickedness.

When he heard God's command, Jonah scowled. Jonah knew that if the Ninevites repented, God would forgive them . . . and that idea sparked outrage in Jonah's heart! He wanted God to pour down His anger and destroy the Ninevites, not show them mercy! Jonah's anger burned so hot that instead of listening to God, he sailed to Tarshish, a city over two thousand miles in the *opposite* direction of Nineveh. In other words, he ran away from God!

Do you think running from God was a good idea or a bad idea?

Jonah should have known he could never escape from God's presence. If he had climbed to heaven, God would be there. If he sank into the middle of the earth, God would be there. As Jonah fled far across the sea, God followed him—and would stop him.

Before long, God hurled a fierce wind upon the sea. The clouds blackened and billowed. Thunder crashed until the sky itself threatened to crack apart. The surf churned so violently that Jonah's ship groaned and creaked, its hull ready to splinter and break.

The sailors on board must have grasped for ropes and yanked the sails tight. They hurled cargo overboard so the weight wouldn't drag them to the murky bottom of the sea. Over and over, they cried out for mercy.

Meanwhile, Jonah *slept* below the deck. He wouldn't pray to God or listen to Him. He didn't even help the sailors whose lives he'd endangered.

The sailors woke Jonah, and he begrudgingly admitted he was running from the God who made the sea and dry land. "What shall we do?" the crew cried in terror.

"Pick me up and hurl me into the sea," Jonah finally said. "It's my fault this storm has happened, and the sea will quiet down if you throw me overboard."

The sailors didn't want Jonah to drown, so they tried to row harder. Still the sea raged and roiled, the winds whipped and whirled, and thunder boomed. Finally, after begging God for forgiveness, the sailors tossed Jonah into the sea with a mighty heave. *SPLASH!*

The instant Jonah struck the water, the ocean stilled. The wind calmed. The clouds melted away like snow on a spring day, and the sun beamed through.

Jonah gasped for breath in the water. Would God leave him to sink to the depths? Would he punish him for his disobedience?

Think about all God had done for His people. How do you think God would treat Jonah?

Jonah had run from God . . . but God wouldn't abandon Jonah! He sent an enormous fish to save Jonah as he sank down, down, down into the sea. The fish opened its gigantic mouth, and *GULP!* It swallowed Jonah whole!

For three days and three nights, Jonah wallowed in the darkness and dank of the fish's belly.

What might Jonah have smelled and heard?

Finally, while locked in that murk, Jonah prayed to God, who had shown him so much mercy. "Salvation belongs to the LORD!" Jonah said.

Finally, the fish spat Jonah out onto dry land—*PTOOEY!* "Now go to Nineveh!" God told Jonah yet again.

This time Jonah listened! He walked throughout the streets of Nineveh and cried, "God will overthrow the city in forty days!"

When the king of Nineveh heard Jonah's warning, he dressed in sackcloth to show his sadness. He commanded all his kingdom not to eat or drink to show they were sorry for the wicked things they'd done. When God saw how the Ninevites humbled themselves, He beautifully and mercifully forgave them!

God had rescued Jonah from the belly of the fish after three days. Hundreds of years later, the Lord would free another prophet—the greatest Prophet—from the heart of the earth after three days. And that Prophet would command even the raging waters to be still.

- Talk with a grown-up about what mercy means. Then count all the times God showed mercy in this story.

  More of the Story—Read Psalm 139:7–10. Can we ever escape from God?

- Read Matthew 12:39–41. How does the story of Jonah foreshadow the Savior?

To whom can you tell this story today?

Illustrations by Mark Cowden

16

The Fiery Furnace

Daniel 1:1–7, 17–20; 3

After they destroyed Jerusalem, the Babylonians dragged many survivors from Judah away in chains. Their tears must have pattered to the earth as they trudged away from their beloved home. And yet God walked with His people even then. He walked with them all the way to the distant walls of Babylon.

Nebuchadnezzar, the king of Babylon, invited three smart young men from Judah to live in the palace. Called Shadrach, Meshach, and Abednego, they were so wise and fair that the king soon made them leaders in his court, which made Nebuchadnezzar's other officials jealous. While these three young men served faithfully, the officials wanted to destroy them . . . and soon, they saw their chance.

Nebuchadnezzar built a gold statue that towered ninety feet high, and he commanded all the kingdom to bow down and worship what he had made. Anyone who didn't bow down to the statue would face death in a fiery furnace!

Shadrach, Meshach, and Abednego knew they couldn't obey the king's command. How could they worship a powerless, mindless statue, when they knew the living God? Their ancestors had made the same mistake in the wilderness, with catastrophic results! No, they couldn't bow down. They *wouldn't* bow down.

Nebuchadnezzar's jealous officials saw their chance!

"O king, live forever!" they said to Nebuchadnezzar. "These men, O king, pay no attention to you; they do not serve your gods or worship the golden image that you have set up."

This news enraged Nebuchadnezzar! "If you do not worship," he warned Shadrach, Meshach, and Abednego, "you shall immediately be cast into a burning fiery furnace! And who is the god who will deliver you out of my hands?"

What a terrifying threat!

What do you think the young men did? Run? Cry? Bow down?

Shadrach, Meshach, and Abednego remembered God's faithfulness, and they stayed strong. "Our God whom we serve is able to deliver us from the burning fiery furnace, and he will deliver us out of your hand, O king," they said. "But if not, be it known to you, O king, that we will not serve your gods or worship the golden image that you have set up."

Those words sealed their fate. In a fury, Nebuchadnezzar ordered the furnace to be heated seven times hotter than usual! The fire was so hot that it burned anyone who came near it! Then, under Nebuchadnezzar's orders, soldiers tied up the three men and hurled them into the furnace.

Nebuchadnezzar watched, peering into the fire in anticipation. Suddenly, his eyes widened, and he rose from his seat in astonishment. "Did we not cast three men bound into the fire?" he cried. "I see four men unbound, walking in the midst of the fire, and they are not hurt. And the appearance of the fourth is like a son of the gods!" In amazement, Nebuchadnezzar rushed to the furnace and called out to Shadrach, Meshach, and Abednego. "Servants of the Most High God! Come out and come here!"

And out they came, completely untouched! The heat of the furnace, which had killed men just at the entrance, had not singed a single hair on their heads. No ashes dirtied their clothes. They didn't even smell like smoke.

God had saved them!

"Blessed be the God of Shadrach, Meshach, and Abednego, who has sent his angel and delivered his servants, who trusted in him!" Nebuchadnezzar declared. "There is no god who is able to rescue this way!"

No God, except one. No God, except the one who was there in the beginning.

God did not leave His people when He guided them through the wilderness as a pillar of fire. He didn't leave them even in Babylon.

And He would send His Savior to walk with them for all time and to rescue them from the fires of sin and death.

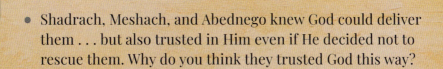

- Shadrach, Meshach, and Abednego knew God could deliver them . . . but also trusted in Him even if He decided not to rescue them. Why do you think they trusted God this way?

- Who do you think was the fourth man in the fiery furnace?

More of the Story—Read Psalm 34:1–8. How do these verses relate to this story?

To whom can you tell this story today?

Illustrations by Alisha Monnin

17

Stone by Stone

Ezra 1; 3:8–13; 4:7–24; Nehemiah 1; 2:1–8; 8:1–8; 13

For seventy years, God's people suffered in Babylon. People called them Jews, as Nebuchadnezzar had forced them from their home in the kingdom of Judah. Meanwhile, that home—the Promised Land into which God had guided them—was ruined and abandoned. Even the glorious temple King David's son had built to worship the Lord now littered the ground in broken pieces.

But God hadn't abandoned His people.

Eventually, the mighty kingdom of Babylon fell to an even mightier power, Persia, and God inspired the new Persian king to free the Jews. "Let all God's people go up to Jerusalem to rebuild the house of the LORD," King Cyrus decreed. Not only did he free the Jews to return to Jerusalem, but he also gave back all the treasures Nebuchadnezzar had stolen! He prepared the Israelites with all the supplies and animals they needed for the long, hard journey home.

The people packed up all their belongings, loaded them onto neighing horses and braying donkeys and groaning camels, and then trekked over long, lonely miles. They trudged for days, that turned into weeks, that turned into months. Finally, after a grueling journey of nine hundred miles, the people glimpsed their beloved home!

They arrived at last to find the temple in ruins and the buildings burned to the ground. Their once treasured, magnificent home was devastated!

What feelings do you think swirled in their hearts as they passed through the rubble?

Swallowing their grief, they set to work rebuilding the temple. They bent their backs and wiped their faces as they labored. Once they built the first layer, the priests blew trumpets in praise, but some of the people wept. How plain this new foundation was, compared to the grand temple that once glittered with gold and reached toward heaven!

The cries of the people echoed across the land, alerting other nations to the work in Jerusalem. And these other nations didn't like it. Not one bit! When a new king ruled Persia, these enemies convinced him to order the Jews to stop building! And so the Jews had to leave their tools and their stones. The dust settled. For eighteen more years the temple lay abandoned and unfinished.

But God hadn't abandoned them! He sent two prophets, Haggai and Zechariah, to encourage the people, and then God worked in the heart of a new king to allow the building to resume. Free to work again, the people built and built until finally, at long last, the temple rose heavenward!

Still, the city wasn't complete. Although the temple shone like a jewel on the horizon, the walls around the city remained crumbled. For seventy years, the people in Jerusalem worshipped in the new temple but feared attacks from enemies.

But still, God hadn't abandoned His people! Back in Persia, a Jewish man named Nehemiah served as the royal cupbearer. When he heard that the city of his ancestors lay in ruins, Nehemiah wept and asked the king for permission to return to Jerusalem to rebuild the wall. The Lord softened the king's heart, and he said yes! Nehemiah traveled to Jerusalem, and under his leadership, the Jews rebuilt the wall of the city in just fifty-two days!

After Jerusalem finally stood again, the people gathered together to listen to the priest Ezra read from God's Word. They bowed down and worshipped the Lord, vowing to follow His commandments always. Yes, they would remember all He had done! Yes, they would follow His ways!

Do you think they did?

Oh, no. The seed of sin still lurked in their hearts. In just a few years, the people were breaking God's laws again and doing what was right in their own eyes. In every green valley, scorching desert, and shady forest, people stole and lied, murdered and hurt one another. Their every thought turned toward evil.

God's people *still* needed a savior! Oh, when would He come?

The people waited and waited for a message from God. Surely He would send another prophet.

They waited and waited and *waited*.

For four hundred years, they waited. But they heard only silence.

- Did God keep His promise to return a remnant to Jerusalem? Count the promises God has kept so far!

- For four hundred years, God didn't send any prophets! Do you think He forgot His people? Why or why not?

More of the Story—Even though God had saved His people from Babylon, they went on sinning. What does this teach you about sin? Hint: read Romans 3:23.

Illustrations by Wazza Pink

The Savior in the Manger

Matthew 1; Luke 1:26–38; 2:1–21

Four hundred years passed without a word from God. The longer the silence stretched on, the deeper God's people sank into ruin.

Roman soldiers soon conquered Judah and renamed it Judea, and once again God's people suffered. The leaders and priests who should have guided the people loved themselves more than God. And while the people struggled, the silence went on and on and on. No prophet brought a message of hope.

But God had not forgotten His people. One astonishing night, He sent the best message of all time to the last person anyone ever expected.

To whom do you think God finally sent His message? To a powerful king? To an important teacher, a general of an army, or even a priest?

Oh no, friend. God's ways are not our ways. After four hundred years, God spoke not to a royal, to a warrior, or even to a rich man, but to a humble young woman named Mary. Although she had descended from King David, Mary wasn't important according to the world. She didn't parade around in rich, jewel-studded robes. Her father hadn't conquered nations or won battles. But God chose her; and like David the shepherd boy, Mary loved and trusted in Him.

God sent His angel Gabriel to Mary. "Greetings, O favored one, the Lord is with you!" the angel said. "Behold, you will conceive in your womb and bear a son, and of his kingdom there will be no end."

How could this be? Although Mary was engaged to a man named Joseph, she wasn't yet married. How could she have a child? And how could she, who was so poor and meek, give birth to a king? Gabriel explained that the baby would be the Son of God Himself! Mary trusted and rejoiced, and soon enough, a baby grew in her womb.

Several months later, when Mary was heavy with child, the emperor commanded all people to return to their birthplaces so his officials might count all the people in his empire. And so, Joseph, Mary, and all their family traveled to Bethlehem, the home of Joseph's ancestors . . . and the place where the prophet Micah said the Savior would be born.

While in Bethlehem, the time came for Mary to give birth, and finally, at long last, after all the long years, the promised Savior entered the world!

He didn't come on a golden chariot or on the back of a lashing wind.

He didn't come with a raised sword or in a column of fire.

Instead, He came as a ruddy, helpless baby. Mary wrapped Him in swaddling cloths and then laid Him not in a bed covered with gold, but in the only place available—a manger. The King of the world lay nestled in the animals' feeding trough. As the angel Gabriel had told them to do, Mary and Joseph named the baby *Jesus*, which means "God saves," because this child would save people from their sins.

That night, a group of shepherds tending their sheep looked up in alarm. An angel appeared before them, his robes like lightning! "Fear not, for behold, I bring you good news of great joy!" the angel said. "For unto you is born this day in the city of Bethlehem a Savior, who is Christ the Lord. And this will be a sign for you: you will find a baby wrapped in swaddling cloths and lying in a manger." Then, before the shepherds' eyes, the sky shone with angels who filled the night with praise. "Glory to God in the highest, and on earth peace among those with whom he is pleased!"

The angels swept away into heaven, and the shepherds looked at one another in amazement. They rushed to Bethlehem, where they discovered Mary, Joseph, and the baby lying in a manger—just as the angel had said.

The Savior had come! At long last, God had sent the King. The Rescuer. The One whose coming the prophets had predicted. The One who would crush the head of the serpent had entered the world!

At long last, God's own firstborn Son had come to dwell among the people—and to save them.

- Mary couldn't understand how God would give her a child, yet she trusted Him. Can you name other people from the Bible who trusted God in mysterious circumstances?

- Why do you think Jesus was born in such a humble place?

More of the Story—Read Psalm 31:21–24. The Jews waited for centuries for the Savior to arrive, but He did, just as God had promised! How does this story guide us?

To whom can you tell this story today?

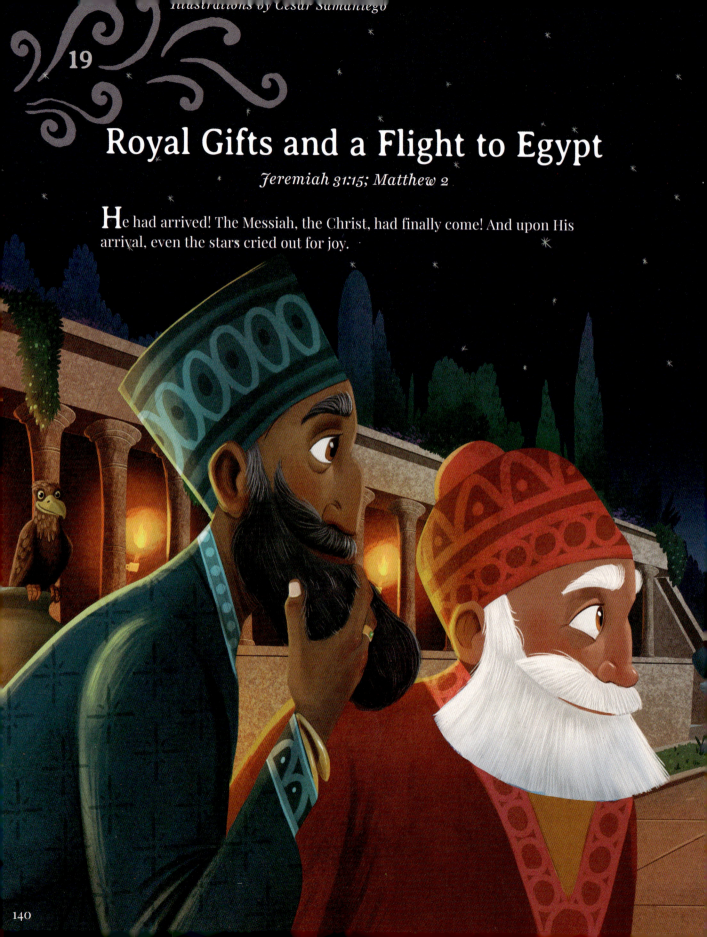

19

Royal Gifts and a Flight to Egypt

Jeremiah 31:15; Matthew 2

He had arrived! The Messiah, the Christ, had finally come! And upon His arrival, even the stars cried out for joy.

After Jesus's birth, a group of wise men living far to the east of Israel glimpsed an extraordinary new star blazing in the night sky. These men studied mathematics, astronomy, and history, and they knew this star meant the birth of a king. Not just any king—a king worthy of worship. So when they saw the star like a beacon in the night, they packed their belongings and journeyed hundreds of miles to Jerusalem to honor the new king.

"Where is he who has been born king of the Jews?" they asked when they reached the city. "For we saw his star when it rose and have come to worship him."

Rather than celebration, the wise men's questions stirred up unease throughout Jerusalem. A king of the Jews? But Israel already had a king—Herod, a king chosen by *Rome*! When Herod heard the rumors, he summoned the chief priests and scribes and asked where the Savior was to be born. When they repeated Micah's prophecy about Bethlehem, Herod called the wise men to him in secret. "Go and search diligently for the child," he said, "and when you have found him, bring me word, that I too may come and worship him."

The wise men journeyed on, and the star blazed ahead of them, guiding them from the sky until it came to rest over the place where Jesus and His family lived. As its light shined on the home, the wise men rejoiced!

They entered, found the child in Mary's arms, and then bowed down to worship Him. After they raised their heads, they unwrapped their bundles and presented the child with royal gifts: precious gold, a perfume called frankincense, and a spice called myrrh. These treasures were more than just pretty gifts: the glittery gold honored His kingship; the fragrant frankincense symbolized the power of God in Him; and myrrh, an embalming spice, forecasted Jesus's death—a death that would change the world. The wise men gave extraordinary gifts for an extraordinary child.

After they worshipped, the men journeyed back home. A dream warned them away from Jerusalem, and so they chose another path. Something was wrong in Herod's palace.

And indeed, something was. A terrible evil had awoken. Herod, who jealously clung to his power, intended not to worship Jesus but to murder Him! When the wise men didn't return, he flew into a rage that boiled over. In a fury, he decreed that soldiers find and kill all boys around Jesus's age who lived near Bethlehem. If Herod couldn't locate the child, then he would kill *all* the boys to make sure none of them threatened his throne!

After all these years, would the Savior die when He was still a child? Would God's plan to save us from our sins fail after all?

Oh, no. God provided for His Son, just as He provides for us.

After the wise men left, an angel of the Lord appeared to Joseph in a dream. "Rise! Take the child and his mother!" the angel warned. "Flee to Egypt, and remain there until I tell you, for Herod is about to search for the child, to destroy him!"

What terrible news! Joseph listened to the warning and awakened Mary. Under the cover of night, they fled to Egypt.

As they left, soldiers stormed into Bethlehem, and cries of mourning soon echoed throughout the town . . . just as they had in Egypt long ago, when Pharaoh's cruelty wrenched newborn babies from their mothers' arms. During that time, God had saved a helpless baby, Moses, who would become a prophet and save his people.

And now, again in Egypt, God protected a prophet even greater than Moses. He was the Messiah, Jesus, who would save the world.

- Although the wise men weren't Jewish, they knew Jesus was the foretold king. What does this tell you about God's message?

- Many of the stories in the Old Testament foreshadow Jesus's coming. With the help of a grown-up, think of some examples.

More of the Story—Jeremiah had prophesied about Herod killing the children in Bethlehem. Read Jeremiah 31:15 and discuss it with a grown-up.

Illustrations by Clara Anganuzzi

20

The River and the Dove

Matthew 3; Mark 1:1–11; Luke 2:52; 3:1–22; John 1:19–34; Acts 19:4

After King Herod died, an angel appeared to Joseph to tell him all was safe, and he and Mary returned to their hometown of Nazareth. As the years passed, Jesus grew in wisdom and stature and favor with God and man, and He astounded others with His understanding of God's Word. The Messiah was ready to begin His ministry!

Before He began, however, God sent one last prophet—the final prophet—to prepare people's hearts. He was called John the Baptist, and he lived a difficult life. To remind himself of his sins, John clothed himself in camel's hair that itched and scratched him. To remind himself of his dependence on God, he ate locusts and wild honey he gathered from the wilderness. John humbly spent his days baptizing people in the Jordan River, washing them with water as a sign of their own need for God to cleanse them of their sins. "Repent, for the kingdom of heaven is at hand!" John would cry, calling to all who could hear.

At this time, the most important people in Judea were the Pharisees, who were scribes, and the Sadducees, who were priests and wealthy officials. Although they had the gift of God's Word, they cared more about looking righteous than about having righteous hearts. They used their knowledge of the law to belittle others, all while puffing themselves up. In other words, they loved themselves more than God.

Many of the Pharisees and Sadducees came to the river to observe John, but they never stepped into the water themselves. They saw themselves as already righteous and clean . . . but John saw differently. "You brood of vipers!" he scolded them. "Who warned you to flee from the wrath to come? Every tree that does not bear good fruit is cut down and thrown into the fire."

At such bold words, the people murmured and whispered to each other about John. "Is he the Christ?" they asked. "Is he the one God has promised to send us?"

"I am not," John said. "After me comes one who is mightier than I, the strap of whose sandals I am not worthy to stoop down and untie. I have baptized you with water, but he will baptize you with the Holy Spirit."

Then, one day, the very person John preached about stepped onto the riverbank of the Jordan. John paused from his baptizing. He raised his head and perhaps lifted a hand to shield his eyes from the glare of the sun on the water. Can you imagine how he drew in a breath when he saw Jesus standing there beside the river?

How fast do you think John's heart must have sped?

Jesus asked John to baptize Him, but John was amazed. "I need to be baptized by you, and do you come to me?" John asked.

But Jesus answered him, "Let it be so now, for thus it is fitting for us to fulfill all righteousness." Although Jesus had never sinned and so didn't *need* to be baptized, He came to live the life Adam—and all of us—should have lived.

And so, John agreed. How his hands must have trembled! God had already told John that he would recognize the Messiah when he saw the Holy Spirit come down from heaven and touch Him. Was this the one?

When Jesus emerged from the water, the heavens tore open! Light cascaded down onto the glittering water, and the Holy Spirit drifted down onto Jesus in the form of a dove. Then God's voice came from heaven: "You are my beloved Son; with you I am well pleased."

The sign God had promised John was right there above the water. God's own firstborn Son had come at last and was ready for the Lord's work!

Jesus's work of saving us had begun!

- A great mystery of God is that He is a trinity—three in persons, one in essence. This story reveals all three persons of the Trinity: God the Father, God the Son, and God the Holy Spirit. Talk with a grown-up about what Jesus's baptism teaches us about the Trinity.

- Why would Jesus have to live a perfect life to save us?

More of the Story—What is the role of the Holy Spirit? Hint: read John 14:26.

To whom can you tell this story today?

Illustrations by Aedan Peterson

21

Temptation in the Wilderness

Psalm 145:15; Matthew 4; Luke 4

After Jesus's baptism, the Holy Spirit led Him into the wilderness for forty days. Just as God's people had wandered for forty years in the wilderness, suffered hunger and thirst, and then sinned horribly against God, so also Jesus would wander, would hunger and thirst . . . and would be tempted to sin. But would He give in?

What would He do, as He trudged through the dust beneath the unforgiving sun? Would He forget God's goodness, as God's own people had done so many times long ago, and so many times since? Would He grumble for food and water? Would He worship created things instead of the Creator of heaven and earth? Would He disobey God?

What do you think Jesus did?

For forty days and forty nights, Jesus ate nothing. As He wandered, His stomach must have twisted with hunger, and dizziness must have made the ground wobble around Him. Then, at the moment when He was most drained and weary, Satan tempted Him just as he had enticed Adam and Eve so long ago.

"If you are the Son of God," Satan said, "command these stones to become loaves of bread."

What would Jesus do?

As had been the case for His ancestors in the wilderness, His stomach groaned, and He felt faint. But Jesus remembered God's Word. "It is written, 'Man shall not live by bread alone,'" He said, "but by every word that comes from the mouth of God."

Jesus knew that more than bread, more than meat, more even than the sweetest honey, He needed God. He needed the One who gives all people their food in every season.

But Satan didn't give up. He took Jesus to Jerusalem, set Him high on the pinnacle of the temple, and said to Him, "If you are the Son of God, throw yourself down from here, for it is written, 'He will command his angels concerning you, and on their hands they will bear you up, lest you strike your foot against a stone.'"

Now Satan was twisting God's words! Just as he had twisted God's words in the garden to trick Adam and Eve, so now he misused them to trick Jesus.

But Jesus remembered God's truth. "It is said, 'You shall not put the Lord your God to the test,'" He answered, quoting Moses's warning to the people to keep God's commandments.

But Satan still didn't give up! The tempter led Jesus to a hill and showed Him all the kingdoms of the world in a single moment. Fortresses and castles, sprawling cities and palaces high upon cliffs stretched out as far as Jesus could see. The kingdoms shimmered beneath the sun, their stone towers and walls promising riches and power. "All these I will give you, if you will fall down and worship me," Satan said.

What would Jesus do? Satan was offering Him power like God! Adam and Eve ate from the forbidden tree for such a temptation. The people at Babel built their sky-high tower for such glory too. The wicked people in Noah's time wanted to be like God. As did those grumbling in the wilderness. And on and on! In every generation, the temptation to snatch up glory had lured people into destruction.

But Jesus remembered God's Word! "Be gone, Satan!" He said. "For it is written, 'You shall worship the Lord your God, and him only shall you serve.'"

Jesus had defeated Satan!

Can you imagine the great deceiver howling in rage? Upon these words, Satan fled in shame, and angels swept down to care for Jesus. As they tended to God's Son, He likely lay on the ground trembling from hunger and exhaustion . . . and yet, even while His muscles ached and His tongue stuck to the roof of His mouth, Jesus was mightier than all the men ever to be born. He had remained faithful to God where others had failed.

He lived the life we all should have lived.

- According to this story, to what should we turn when we feel tempted to sin?

- How did Jesus live the life that Adam should have? That we all should have?

More of the Story—What words did Jesus use to defeat Satan? Hint: read Deuteronomy 8:3; Deuteronomy 6:16; and Exodus 20:3.

To whom can you tell this story today?

Illustrations by Evelt Yanait

22

The Wondrous Teacher

*Matthew 4:18–22; 9:9–12; 10:1–4; Mark 1:16–20;
Luke 5:1–11; John 1:35–51*

After He returned from the wilderness, Jesus traveled across Israel to bring hope to thousands struggling with sickness, hunger, and sadness over their sin. Along the way, He recruited disciples to follow Him, to learn from Him, and to spread His teachings.

Jesus began in Galilee, a region north of Jerusalem with a lake so huge that people called it a sea. While teaching on the shore one day, He saw two brothers, Simon and Andrew, washing their fishing nets beside their boats. A great crowd pressed in on Jesus to hear His words, so He climbed into Simon's boat and taught from the water, preaching about the coming kingdom when God would finally, at long last, dwell with His people forever.

Afterward, Jesus asked Simon to take the boat a little farther from the shore. "Put out into the deep and let down your nets for a catch," Jesus said.

"Master, we toiled all night and took nothing," Simon said. "But at your word I will let down the nets." Simon unfurled them into the water, and suddenly,

after hours without a single catch, the nets creaked, groaned, and threatened to break from the colossal number of fish squirming inside! Simon and Andrew signaled for help from their friends in a nearby boat. Together the men hauled in nets so overloaded with fish that the boats threatened to sink. As the boats bobbed and rocked, Simon fell down at Jesus's knees. What sort of man was this that He could command the creatures in the sea? "Depart from me, for I am a sinful man, O Lord!" Simon pleaded.

"Do not be afraid," Jesus said. "Follow me, and I will make you fishers of men." In awe, the men headed to shore, and when Jesus left the boat, all of them trailed after Him. Although fishing was their work, Jesus so astounded them that Simon and Andrew left everything—their nets and their boats and the fish wriggling in the weave—to follow Jesus and learn from Him as His disciples.

Days later, Jesus saw a tax collector named Matthew sitting at his booth. People in Israel hated tax collectors because they worked for Rome and often cheated their countrymen out of money to fill their own pockets. What would Jesus do when He approached Matthew? Would He scold him for betraying his own people? Would He shame him for his greed and deceit?

What do you think Jesus did?

Oh, no. He didn't yell at Matthew. Instead, Jesus offered the tax collector an invitation!

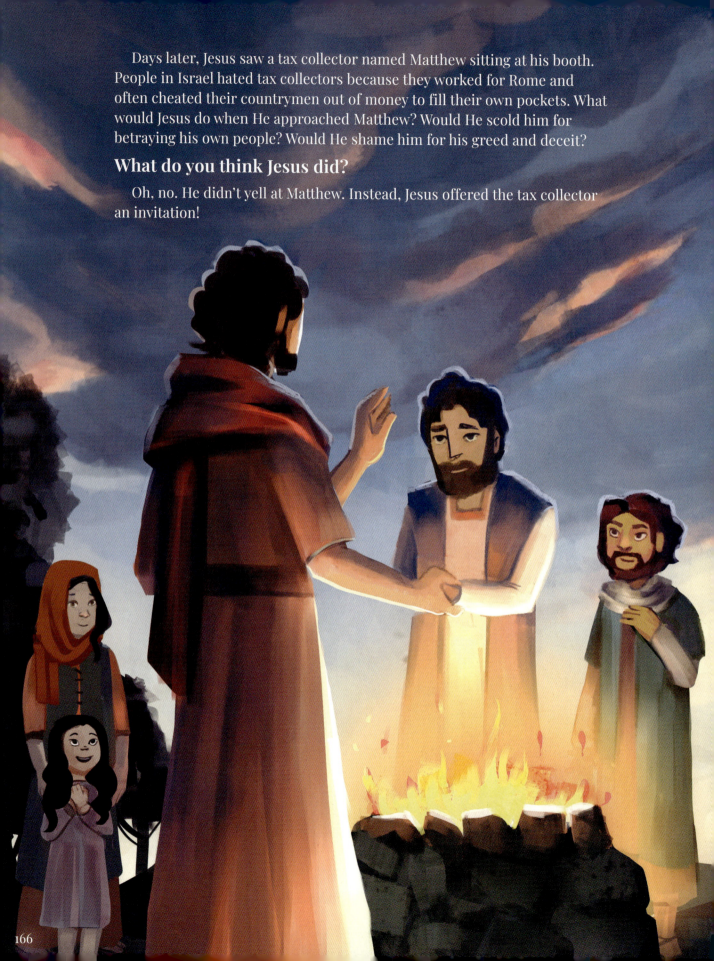

"Follow me," Jesus said, perhaps extending an open hand toward the despised man. And just as with the other disciples, Matthew got up, left everything, and followed! He invited Jesus and the disciples to his home, where he served them dinner. As they dined, more tax collectors and sinners ventured to Matthew's house to hear the words of this wondrous teacher.

When the Pharisees saw the crowd that flocked to Jesus, they scowled. "Why does your teacher eat with tax collectors and sinners?" they asked the disciples.

Jesus heard them. "It is not the healthy who need a doctor, but the sick," He said. Then He quoted to them from the prophet Hosea: "Go and learn what this means: 'I desire mercy, not sacrifice.'" In other words, following the rules perfectly doesn't impress God if we do so with hardened, wicked hearts.

The Pharisees went away grumbling. Who did Jesus think He was, telling them about God's law? Seeds of resentment sprouted within them, and over time, those seeds would grow and grow and grow.

Jesus called more men into His ministry, with a total of twelve set apart as His apostles: Simon (whom Jesus renamed Peter) and Andrew, James and John, Philip and Bartholomew, Thomas and Matthew, James the son of Alphaeus, Judas Thaddeus, Simon the Zealot, and Judas Iscariot. All of them listened to Jesus, and all marveled at the wonders they saw when they were with Him.

But not all loved Him.

One would betray Him. After all the long years waiting for our Savior, one of Jesus's own chosen apostles would hand Him over to His enemies.

And that betrayal would send shockwaves around the world.

- The apostles in this story left everything they had to follow Jesus. What does that tell you about Jesus's importance?

- What does following Jesus look like in your own life?

  More of the Story—Read Luke 6:37. Did the Pharisees uphold this teaching of Jesus? Why not?

Illustrations by Mariano Epelbaum

23

The Prodigal Son

Matthew 10:34; Luke 15:11–32; Ephesians 2:5; Hebrews 4:12

Many people expected the Messiah to come with armor and a flashing sword. They longed for a hero to sweep away the Roman soldiers as God had swept away Pharaoh's chariots in the Red Sea.

Jesus was that hero, but He offered something far more precious than freedom from Rome. Jesus came bearing a sword far sharper than a flashing steel blade: He brought the sword of God's Word.

Jesus often taught through a special type of story called a *parable*. He told one such story to encourage sinners who longed for forgiveness and also to scold the Pharisees and priests.

The story began in the home of a wealthy man with two sons. In those days, sons would inherit their father's possessions upon his death, but this man's youngest son didn't want to wait. He wanted his inheritance *now*. "Father, give me the share of property that is coming to me," he demanded. The father, who was loving and patient, agreed.

171

The younger son soon journeyed to a faraway country, where he wasted all his money. Whether it was on rich food or fancy clothes or jars of the most expensive wine, he spent each and every coin. And with his moneybag empty, his stomach soon grew hollow as well. A famine ruined the land, his muscles wasted away, and he swooned with hunger.

Desperate for money and food, the son found work caring for pigs. His stomach so ached that even the pigs' food seemed appetizing! As he considered how low he had fallen, he remembered how his father, a kind and gentle man, had provided him with his every need.

"How many of my father's hired servants have more than enough bread, but I perish here with hunger!" the son thought. "I will arise and go to my father, and I will say to him, 'Father, I have sinned against heaven and before you. I am no longer worthy to be called your son. Treat me as one of your hired servants.'" And so he stood up, wiped the pigs' slop from his hands, and wearily trudged home.

What would his father say? Would he scold the young son? Would he cast him away and forbid him ever to return?

What do you think the father did?

Oh, dear friend. This father is like our Father—like the Father who made heaven and earth and whose love and faithfulness last forever.

This father had been watching the horizon for his son, aching for him to come home. When at long last the younger son appeared, bedraggled, filthy, and weak, the father didn't raise his voice. He didn't scold or yell. Instead, when he saw his son still a long way off, he ran to him! His heart filled with compassion as he hugged his son and kissed him.

"Bring quickly the best robe!" the father told his servants. "Put it on him, and put a ring on his hand, and shoes on his feet. And bring the fattened calf and kill it, and let us eat and celebrate. For this my son was dead, and is alive again; he was lost, and is found." The household rejoiced!

But one person wasn't happy. Rather than join the celebration, the older brother stomped away and grumbled. When his father came out to ask him why he refused to join, he said, "Look, these many years I have served you, and I never disobeyed your command, yet you never even gave me a young goat that I might celebrate with my friends. But when this son of yours has wasted all your money, you killed the fattened calf for him!"

"Son, you are always with me, and all that is mine is yours," the father said. "It was fitting to celebrate and be glad, for this your brother was dead, and is alive; he was lost, and is found."

So we, too, were dead in our sins and trespasses . . . but are made alive in Christ.

- Remember that Jesus taught this parable both to tax collectors and to the Pharisees. Whom do you think the younger brother symbolizes?

- Whom do you think the older brother represents?

More of the Story—Whom does the father represent? What does this tell you about God? Hint: read Daniel 9:9 and Psalm 86:5.

To whom can you tell this story today?

Illustrations by James Bernardin

24

Miraculous Healings

*Isaiah 35:5–6; Matthew 8:1–17; 9:1–8; 12:9–14;
Mark 1:29–34; 7:31–34; Luke 5:12–26; 8:41–56*

Jesus's work as the Savior wouldn't happen all of a sudden, in a hailstorm of fire or a flash of lightning. Rather, He came to warn sinners to turn back to God and trust in Him. He came to teach the suffering and the broken about God's love for them. And He came to heal the sick and the wounded, to show that as God's own Son He possessed the power to reverse the ugly work of sin and death.

God's laws included many, many rules to make sure the people could be in His holy presence. If people touched someone with a disease, they themselves would be unclean and would become outcasts, forbidden from entering the temple and forced to stay outside the cities.

Amazingly, when Jesus touched people who were sick, instead of becoming unclean Himself, *He cleansed them.* He healed them, just as the prophet Isaiah had predicted when he wrote, "He took our illnesses and bore our diseases." Jesus took them over and over and over.

One day Peter brought Jesus to his house, where Peter's mother-in-law was sick with a fever. When Jesus touched her hand, the fever left her in an instant, and she rose to serve Him.

As word spread of Jesus's miracles, people journeyed from far and wide to see Him. One evening, while Jesus taught inside a house, the crowd around Him was so large that a paralyzed man couldn't squeeze inside. The man's four friends were so desperate for Jesus to heal him that they tore tiles from the roof and lowered their friend down in his bed! When Jesus saw their faith, He offered the suffering man the best healing of all. "Your sins are forgiven," He said.

Instead of being amazed, the scribes and the priests grumbled when they heard Jesus. "Who is this who speaks blasphemies?" they said. "Who can forgive sins but God alone?"

Jesus knew their thoughts. "Which is easier to say, 'Your sins are forgiven,' or to say, 'Rise and walk?'" He asked. "But that you may know that the Son of Man has authority on earth to forgive sins . . ." Then He turned to the paralyzed man and said, "I say to you, rise, pick up your bed, and go home." Immediately the man stood, picked up his mat, and *walked* home, glorifying God all the way!

When the man walked, how do you think his friends reacted? What about the Pharisees?

Another time, a man suffering with leprosy, a terrible disease that causes sores all over the body, fell on his face before Jesus and begged, "Lord, if you will, you can make me clean."

Jesus stretched out His hand and touched the leper, saying, "I will; be clean," and immediately the leprosy left him!

On and on, Jesus's miracles continued. He gave sight to the blind, speech to the mute, and hearing to the deaf. He wiped away leprosy as if it were a coating of dust, and He restored warmth and movement to a man's withered hand. He commanded those whose legs folded stiff and useless beneath them to walk, and they rose. A woman who had bled for twelve years merely touched the fringe of His robe, and Jesus's power flowed into her and healed her. He even bid those who had died to rise again, and they drew breath, their eyes fluttered open, and the blush of life again crept into their cheeks!

These miracles fulfilled what the prophet Isaiah had predicted about the Messiah:

> Then the eyes of the blind shall be opened,
> And the ears of the deaf unstopped;
> Then shall the lame man leap like a deer,
> And the tongue of the mute sing for joy.

Everyone saw what Jesus did and marveled.

Everyone, that is, except the Pharisees and Sadducees, the arrogant scribes and priests. As keepers of God's Word, they should have recognized Jesus as the Messiah. Instead they burned with jealousy and hatred toward Him. As Jesus healed multitudes of the wounded, desperate, and hurting, the teachers of God's law conspired to destroy Him.

- Jesus healed people and made them clean. Who was the source of His power?

- Why were the Pharisees and Sadducees so angry? (Hint: what does "blasphemy" mean?)

More of the Story—Read 1 Peter 2:24, a verse about Jesus. Discuss with a grown-up how Jesus's healing miracles point to His reason for coming to us.

Illustrations by Arief Putra

25

Bread to Feed Thousands

Isaiah 53:6; Matthew 14:13-21; Mark 6:30-44; John 6:1-15, 22-51

The more miracles Jesus performed, the more people flocked to Him. One day the crowds were so overwhelming that Jesus guided His disciples into a boat to break free. They sailed across the sea, but the people followed, racing on foot through all the towns. When Jesus arrived at a quiet mountain where He might teach His disciples in peace, He discovered a multitude of people already waiting for Him. Rather than flee, or scold them, Jesus had compassion. They reminded Him of sheep without a shepherd—lost, wandering far from their loving, heavenly Father. And so Jesus taught them and healed their diseases until dusk cast the sky in a hazy glow.

As evening fell, the disciples encouraged Jesus to send the people home. "This is a desolate place, and the hour is now late," they said. "Send the crowds away to go into the surrounding countryside and villages and buy food for themselves."

"They need not go away," Jesus said. "You give them something to eat."

The disciples scanned the crowd in bewilderment. People teemed over the whole mountainside, with five thousand men, not counting women and children. How could the disciples possibly buy bread for so many?

"How many loaves do you have?" Jesus asked.

"There is a boy here who has five barley loaves and two fish," said Andrew, "but what are they for so many?"

"Have the people sit down," Jesus said.

As He requested, the crowd sat on the grass in groups of hundreds and fifties. Jesus took the five loaves of bread from the boy, gave thanks to God, and broke them. He gave the broken loaves to the disciples to distribute among the people. Around and around the bread went.

Jesus did the same thing with the fish. Around and around it went.

**How quickly do you think the food ran out?
In two minutes? Ten?**

Actually, the food never ran out. Remarkably, everyone on the mountainside ate until they were full! Out of more than five thousand people, not a single belly groaned with hunger. Afterward, the disciples gathered up twelve basketfuls of leftover pieces.

"This is indeed the Prophet who has come into the world!" some of the people cried.

But many didn't truly understand. When Jesus sailed across the sea the next day, crowds chased after Him—not because they longed to know God but because their bellies were again empty. Just like the people in the wilderness, their rumbling stomachs drove their actions.

Jesus saw the sin in their hearts. "Do not work for the food that perishes, but for the food that endures to eternal life, which the Son of Man will give to you," He urged them. But still, they didn't understand.

"Then what sign will you do, that we may see and believe you?" the people said. "What work do you perform? Our fathers ate manna in the wilderness; as it is written, 'He gave them bread from heaven to eat.'"

Jesus gave them nourishment to satisfy their souls, not their appetites. He responded, "I am the bread of life. Whoever comes to me shall never hunger, and whoever believes in me shall never thirst. Truly, truly, I say to you, whoever believes has eternal life. I am the living bread that came down from heaven. And the bread that I will give for the life of the world is my flesh."

At these words, many rejected Jesus. They didn't understand that the only true nourishment came not from dough baked in an oven, but from God's own Son. And they didn't understand that the Savior would have to suffer.

They didn't understand that to save our lives, Jesus would have to give His own.

- What do you think Jesus meant when He said, "I am the bread of life"?

- Did the crowds following Jesus really understand who He was?

More of the Story—Read Deuteronomy 8:3. Jesus quoted from this verse to defeat Satan in the wilderness. How does this same verse relate to this story about feeding the five thousand?

To whom can you tell this story today?

Illustrations by Patrick Corrigan

26

The Storm That Hushed

Matthew 8:23–27; 14:22–33; Mark 4:35–41; John 6:14–21

What sort of man was this mysterious Savior? Jesus healed the sick and the lame. He gave sight to the blind and hearing to the deaf. He fed thousands with just five loaves of bread and two fish.

And as the disciples would learn, He had power even over the sea and sky.

One evening, as daylight slipped away and night seeped across the horizon, Jesus told His disciples to travel by boat with Him across the Sea of Galilee. As the journey across the water wore on and the night deepened, Jesus drifted off to sleep.

To the disciples' dismay, while He slept, storm clouds blotted out the stars, and a fierce wind churned the sea into froth. *WHOOSH!* Waves pummeled the boat and flooded the deck. The disciples scrambled to steady the boat and bail out water, but the sea threatened to swallow them up like a merciless giant gulping its supper whole.

While the disciples cried and clambered, Jesus slept soundly! He lay on a cushion in the stern of the boat, as peaceful as still water on a summer day.

"Save us, Lord! We are perishing!" the disciples shouted.

Jesus awoke and saw the panic in their eyes. What He did next astounded them. "Why are you afraid, O you of little faith?" He said. Then He rose to His feet and faced the raging sea. "Peace! Be still!" He commanded the storm.

Instantly, the winds died away and the sea was as still and flat as a plate of glass! Soon the boat arrived at their destination, gliding gently toward a tranquil shore.

The disciples gaped at Jesus in awe. "What sort of man is this, that even winds and sea obey him?" they whispered to each other.

Another time, crowds rallied to force Jesus to be king. To avoid them, He slipped away up a mountain to pray and instructed the disciples to sail ahead of Him across the Sea of Galilee. By the time evening fell, the boat had sailed far from shore, with the waves and wind beating against them. As they piloted the ship through the choppy seas, suddenly something caught their eye: a figure stood atop the water.

What was it? A seabird? The tail of a great fish?

Oh, no. It was Jesus, walking across the water as if it were a marble floor!
At first, the disciples didn't recognize Him. "It's a ghost!" they cried out in terror.

Jesus replied with the same calm as He had during the storm. "Take heart," He said. "It is I. Do not be afraid."

Peter wanted proof. "Lord, if it is you, command me to come to you on the water."

"Come," Jesus said. So Peter swung one leg over the side of the boat. Then the other.

When Peter stepped on the surface of the waves, perhaps they felt like solid stone beneath his feet. He walked on the water toward Jesus!

As Peter looked around, however, he noticed the wind tossing the sea into waves. Fear filled his heart, and suddenly his feet sank down beneath the surface. "Lord, save me!" he cried out.

What would happen? Would Peter sink?

Jesus reached out His hand and took hold of Peter. "O you of little faith, why did you doubt?" He asked. Then they got into the boat, the wind ceased, and again they arrived beside the shore.

Who was this man? Jesus was flesh and blood, and walked among them, but He commanded the sea as only God had done when He made it shrink back from beneath Moses's staff long, long ago. As only God could do, when He quieted the storming waters and saved Jonah, and when He commanded the floodwaters to recede from the earth.

As these thoughts raced through their minds, the disciples dropped to their knees before Jesus and worshipped Him. "Truly," they said, "you are the Son of God!"

- List all the miracles Jesus has performed so far in this book.

- Only God has power over the wind and the waves. What does Jesus's power tell you about who He is?

More of the Story—Read John 1:1 and 1:14. Discuss with a grown-up the meaning of these verses.

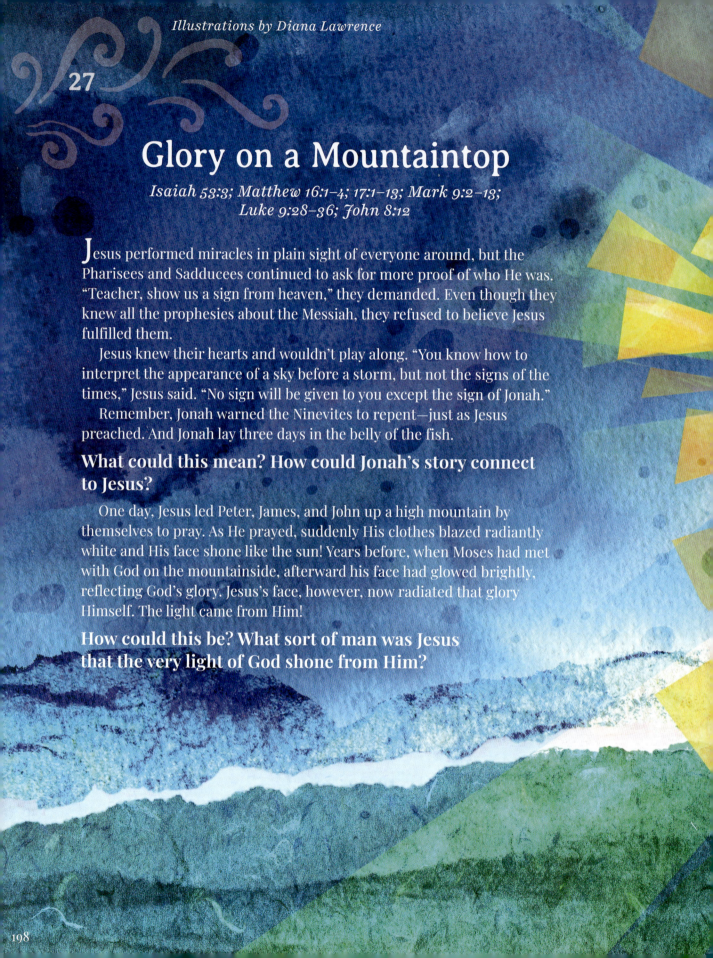

Illustrations by Diana Lawrence

27

Glory on a Mountaintop

Isaiah 53:3; Matthew 16:1–4; 17:1–13; Mark 9:2–13; Luke 9:28–36; John 8:12

Jesus performed miracles in plain sight of everyone around, but the Pharisees and Sadducees continued to ask for more proof of who He was. "Teacher, show us a sign from heaven," they demanded. Even though they knew all the prophesies about the Messiah, they refused to believe Jesus fulfilled them.

Jesus knew their hearts and wouldn't play along. "You know how to interpret the appearance of a sky before a storm, but not the signs of the times," Jesus said. "No sign will be given to you except the sign of Jonah."

Remember, Jonah warned the Ninevites to repent—just as Jesus preached. And Jonah lay three days in the belly of the fish.

What could this mean? How could Jonah's story connect to Jesus?

One day, Jesus led Peter, James, and John up a high mountain by themselves to pray. As He prayed, suddenly His clothes blazed radiantly white and His face shone like the sun! Years before, when Moses had met with God on the mountainside, afterward his face had glowed brightly, reflecting God's glory. Jesus's face, however, now radiated that glory Himself. The light came from Him!

How could this be? What sort of man was Jesus that the very light of God shone from Him?

While Jesus stood in glory, Moses and Elijah appeared! The apostles had been dozing on and off, but when their eyes fluttered open and they saw Jesus's glory and the two men with Him, they jolted to their feet. Peter had no idea what to say or do, and so he bumbled and fumbled with his words. "Master, it is good we are here," he stammered. "Let us make three tents, one for you and one for Moses and one for Elijah."

As Peter spoke, a bright cloud overshadowed them, and a voice thundered out. It was the same voice that had boomed from heaven on the day of Jesus's baptism, when the sky had yawned open and the Holy Spirit had drifted down upon Jesus in the form of a dove. Just as on that day, again God proclaimed His love for Jesus. "This is my beloved Son, with whom I am well pleased; listen to him!"

At the sound of the Father's voice, the apostles fell to their knees, dropped their faces to the ground, and trembled! But as they lay shuddering on the earth, they felt a gentle touch on their shoulders. "Rise, and have no fear," Jesus said. They lifted their eyes, and to their astonishment only Jesus stood before them. The cloud had gone, and the light had faded from Jesus's face. Elijah and Moses had disappeared.

As they came down from the mountain, Jesus warned His disciples not to tell anyone of the marvels they'd seen on the mountaintop until after He had risen from the dead.

Risen from the dead? Whatever could Jesus mean? The disciples knew Jesus was the Messiah, but they still couldn't comprehend what that meant for the days ahead. And what it meant for them.

"Jesus, why do the scribes say that first Elijah must come?" they asked, recalling that the prophet Elijah was to return and prepare the way for the Messiah.

"I tell you that Elijah has come, and they did not recognize him, but did to him whatever they pleased," Jesus said, referring to John the Baptist, whom King Herod had imprisoned. "So also, the Son of Man will certainly suffer at their hands and be treated with contempt."

The apostles had no reply. They still didn't remember the Messiah would be pierced and crushed for our wrongdoings. They didn't grasp that before He freed us from our sins, He would first suffer rejection, hatred, sorrow, and grief. To free us from the chains of death, Jesus would first have to die. He'd have to take the punishment we all deserve for sin.

The apostles listened and sealed their lips, although their hearts likely burned to share what they'd seen. The time to retell this remarkable story had not yet come.

But it would come, much sooner than they realized.

- What did Jesus mean by the sign of Jonah?

More of the Story—Why do you think Elijah and Moses appeared on the mountain? Hint: read Luke 24:44.

Read Isaiah 53:4–5. What do these verses tell us about what the Messiah would have to do?

To whom can you tell this story today?

Illustrations by Ana Latese

28

Lazarus Raised

John 1:1–3, 14; 11

The more Jesus spoke about being God's Son, the more the chief priests' anger smoldered. "Who does this man think he is, to call himself the Son of God?" they protested. They tried to arrest Him. They gathered crowds to stone Him. But with each threat, Jesus slipped away to remote places and escaped them.

And still, even while danger mounted, Jesus performed wonders and preached good news to the heartbroken.

After a crowd near Jerusalem tried to stone Him, Jesus retreated to the banks of the Jordan River. While there, He received troubling news about His dear friend Lazarus in the town of Bethany: "Lord, he whom you love is ill."

Lazarus's sisters, Martha and Mary, hoped Jesus would rush to their brother's side to heal him. Jesus had cured strangers with just a word or a touch of His hand; surely He would rescue His dear friend?

What would you have expected Jesus to do?

When Jesus received their message, however, He stayed where He was for two days. Only after this delay did He tell the disciples to pack for the journey to Bethany, close to Jerusalem.

The disciples looked at one another worriedly. "Teacher, the Jews were just seeking to stone you, and you are going there again?" they said.

"Our friend Lazarus has fallen asleep, but I go to awaken him," Jesus said.

The disciples didn't understand. "Lord, if he has fallen asleep, he will recover."

"Lazarus has died," Jesus said plainly. "And for your sake I am glad I was not there, that you may believe. But let us go to him."

They arrived after Lazarus had already been buried in a tomb for four days. When Martha heard Jesus was near, she rushed out to meet Him on the road. "Lord, if you had been here, my brother would not have died. But even now I know that whatever you ask from God, God will give you."

How do you think Martha felt? Can you imagine the tender look Jesus must have given her?

205

"Your brother will rise again," Jesus said. "I am the resurrection and the life. Whoever believes in me, though he die, yet shall he live, and everyone who lives and believes in me shall never die."

Then Mary raced down the road to meet Jesus and fell at His feet. "Lord, if you had been here, my brother would not have died," she said between sobs.

When Jesus saw Mary weeping, along with the crowds of mourners who followed her, His spirit was greatly troubled. "Where have you laid him?" He asked. When they took Him to the tomb, Jesus wept too.

"See, how he loved him!" the onlookers remarked.

Yet even after seeing Jesus's compassion, some muttered: "He opened the eyes of the blind man. Couldn't he also have kept this man from dying?"

Jesus approached the tomb, its entrance sealed with a rock. "Take away the stone," He said.

Martha hesitated. "Lord, by this time there will be an odor, for he has been dead four days."

"Did I not tell you that if you believed you would see the glory of God?" Jesus said. So they took away the stone, and Jesus lifted His eyes. "Father, I thank you that you have heard me. I knew that you always hear me, but I said this on account of the people standing around, that they may believe that you sent me." Then He cried out in a loud voice, "Lazarus, come out!"

All the crowd gasped! Lazarus, dead for four days, walked out from the tomb, his hands and feet still bound in linen strips and his face wrapped with a cloth. Jesus said to them, "Unbind him, and let him go."

The people standing around marveled! Many in the crowd that day placed their faith in Jesus. But some reported Jesus's actions to the Pharisees. From that day forward, the chief priests and scribes plotted to kill Jesus. Jesus, our Savior, who committed no sin.

Jesus, the Son of the living God.

- How does this story reveal who Jesus is?

- Why did Jesus wait before traveling to see Lazarus?

More of the Story—Read Genesis 50:20 and Romans 8:28. What do those verses and this story teach us about God's work when difficult things happen in life?

To whom can you tell this story today?

Illustrations by Leo Trinidad

29

The King on the Donkey

Matthew 21:1–11; Mark 11:1–11; Luke 19:28–48; John 12:12–19

Jesus was no ordinary hero. He came not with a shield and a war horse but wrapped in swaddling clothes and lying in a manger. He healed sicknesses and brought the dead to life. He held power over the wind and the waves. And on a mountain with His disciples, he radiated God's glory.

Jesus could do all this *because He was God.*

In the greatest mystery of all time, God lowered Himself and took on human flesh. Jesus was God's own Son, one with the Father, with Him in the very beginning when light first blazed through the darkness. He had appeared in the burning bush to Moses and in the fiery furnace in Babylon. The Savior for whom all generations waited was God Himself. God the Son came to save us!

But that salvation would come at a terrible price.

When the chief priests and the Pharisees were actively scheming to destroy Him, Jesus set His eyes toward Jerusalem for one last time. "Go into the village in front of you," He told His disciples, "and immediately you will find a donkey colt that has never been ridden. Untie it and bring it to me. If anyone says anything to you, you shall say, 'The Lord needs it.'"

The disciples did as Jesus directed and found a donkey and her colt tied outside a doorway. "What are you doing, untying that colt?" people asked as the disciples unwound the ropes. They repeated what Jesus had instructed, and sure enough the people left them alone. Then the disciples laid their cloaks across the colt's back, and Jesus climbed on and rode into the city.

How easy do you think it is to ride a donkey that's never had someone on its back before? What does this tell you about Jesus's authority?

Now, on a donkey's colt, Jesus the King entered Jerusalem. His arrival fulfilled the prophecy of Zechariah: "Fear not, daughter of Zion; behold, your king is coming, sitting on a donkey's colt!"

As He plodded along—*CLOMP, CLOMP, CLOMP*—crowds who had traveled to the city for the Passover gathered by the road to welcome Him as king. Some spread their cloaks on the ground. Others cut palm branches from trees in the fields and laid them on the road before Jesus. All around, people shouted, "Hosanna to the Son of David! Blessed is he who comes in the name of the Lord, even the King of Israel! Hosanna in the highest!"

When the chief priests heard the people proclaiming Jesus as the Messiah, they reddened with fury. "Teacher, rebuke your disciples!" they demanded.

"I tell you," Jesus said, "if these were silent, the very stones would cry out."

Jesus's arrival stirred up the whole city. Potters paused at their wheels.

Women stopped their kneading to listen. Sellers and buyers paused in the markets, their arms still outstretched to pass money or purchased pieces of fruit. Men, women, and children spilled into the streets to behold the source of the clamor. "Who is this?" they asked.

And the answer came: "This is the prophet Jesus, from Nazareth of Galilee!"

This was Jesus, God's own Son, who came to save us!

Jesus rode to the temple and entered to find not the hush of prayer but the clink of coins and the bleats and tweets of animals. Bankers, traders, and salespeople had taken over God's house for themselves, selling sacrificial animals and filching money from the poor in a space meant for people to worship. In their greed, these sellers had robbed people the chance to draw closer to God!

The sight of such wickedness kindled Jesus's anger, and sellers staggered back as He overturned the stands. Pigeons flew away—*FLAP, FLAP, FLAP*—in a flurry of feathers. Tables toppled over, and coins clattered across the stones. "It is written, my house shall be called a house of prayer, but you make it a den of robbers!" Jesus cried, and He drove the sellers out of the temple!

Still the crowds followed Him. The blind and the lame flocked to Him, pleading for mercy. Children cried out, "Hosanna to the Son of David!" Through it all, the chief priests and scribes scowled, frowned, and plotted to kill Him. To succeed, they'd recruit the help of one of Jesus's very own apostles.

- What kind of king did the people expect the Messiah to be?

- What kind of king did the prophets say the Messiah would be?

More of the Story—The people called Jesus the "Son of David." Read God's promise to David in 2 Samuel 7:16–17. How does Jesus fulfill this promise?

Illustrations by Chiara Fedele

30

Tears in the Garden

Matthew 26:14-46; Luke 22:1-23; John 13:21-30

Even while Jesus preached about the kingdom of God, Satan was at work. He slithered into the minds of men and coaxed the seed of sin in their hearts to bloom. And he spoke especially sinister words to Judas Iscariot.

Judas was one of Jesus's twelve apostles. He was greedy, pocketing the disciples' money for himself. He loved money more than God, and for the sake of that love he betrayed God's own Son.

Judas met with the chief priests in secret. "What will you give me if I deliver Jesus over to you?" he asked.

The priests must have grinned maliciously. After all their efforts to arrest Jesus, at last, this was their chance! They promised Judas thirty pieces of silver—the price of a slave—and they schemed about how Judas would betray Jesus. They plotted to arrest Him when He was alone, so no crowd could stop them. "The one I kiss is the man," Judas said. "Seize him."

Why do you think Judas betrayed Jesus?

Soon the Passover arrived. Jesus and His disciples prepared a meal of lamb, unleavened bread, and bitter herbs, just as God had commanded so long ago. It would be the last supper they would share together.

At the table, Jesus picked up the bread, gave thanks, and broke it before giving it to His disciples. He said, "Take, eat; this is my body, which is given for you. Do this in remembrance of me."

Then He took a cup of wine and said, "Drink of it, all of you, for this is my blood of the covenant, which is poured out for many for the forgiveness of sins." The disciples did as He said, although His words confused them. Then Jesus said something shocking: "One of you will betray me."

What? Who could betray Jesus, the Christ, who'd worked wonders and taught them the ways of God? Who could betray the One who was God Himself? "Is it I, Lord?" they asked, one after another.

"He who has dipped his hand in the dish with me will betray me," Jesus said. Then He dipped a piece of bread into a bowl of wine or meat juice and gave it to Judas Iscariot. "What you are going to do, do quickly," Jesus said. Others around the table thought Jesus was asking Judas to purchase food for the feast, but at His words Judas rose from the table and fled from the room.

After they ate, Jesus went to the Mount of Olives, a mountain where He'd often preached and prayed. The disciples followed Him, and as they walked He continued to speak words that troubled and astonished them. "You will all fall away because of me this night," Jesus said.

"I will never fall away!" Peter protested.

But Jesus said, "I tell you, Peter, this very night, before the rooster crows, you will deny me three times."

How do you think Peter felt in that moment? Have you ever done something you promised you wouldn't?

When they reached a garden called Gethsemane, Jesus asked Peter, James, and John to go on with Him in private. "My soul is very sorrowful, even to death," He said, His head hung low, and His shoulders stooped with grief. "Remain here and watch with me." Then He walked about a stone's throw away from them, where He fell to the ground and prayed, saying, "Father, if you are willing, remove this cup from me. Nevertheless, not my will, but yours be done." He prayed the same prayer three times. So great was His sorrow that His sweat darkened with beads of blood!

Yet while Jesus agonized, the disciples dozed off to sleep. "You could not watch with me one hour?" Jesus said, waking them. "Sleep and take your rest later on. See, the hour is at hand."

Just then, He must have heard the tromping of feet and the clink of armor coming nearer. Temple guards marched into the garden, torchlight glinting off blades in their hands.

At the head of them, his eyes fixed on Jesus, was Judas Iscariot.

- What did Jesus mean by the bread and the wine? How do we now remember His words in church?

- How did Jesus pray to the Father? How can this guide us in our own prayers?

More of the Story—John the Baptist called Jesus "the Lamb of God, who takes away the sin of the world" (John 1:29). How is Jesus like the lambs from the first Passover in Egypt?

Illustrations by Monique Steele

31

The Terrible Betrayal

Matthew 26:27–45; 27:11–31; Luke 22:47–71; 23:1–25; John 18:1–32; 19:1–16

Judas had seen Jesus feed multitudes, heal the sick, calm the storm, and raise Lazarus from death. But the seed of sin still lurked in Judas's heart—just as it has lurked in every heart since Adam and Eve, every heart except Jesus's. And so Judas stepped forward with a throng of temple guards armed with swords, and he betrayed the Son of God.

"Greetings, Rabbi!" Judas said. Then he betrayed Jesus with a kiss.

The kiss signaled the soldiers to surge forward to arrest Jesus. "Lord, shall we strike with the sword?" the disciples cried out, rushing to protect Him. Peter even swung his blade and sliced off the right ear of the high priest's servant.

"No more of this!" Jesus said. "Put your sword back in its place!" He reached out His hand and touched the servant's wound, and suddenly the ear was healed and like new! Then the mob swarmed forward, and the soldiers grabbed Jesus and tied His hands. The disciples, who had pledged to follow Him always, ran away in terror.

As the soldiers towed Jesus into the house of Caiaphas, the high priest, Peter followed from a distance then sat by a fire in the courtyard to warm himself. As he leaned into the blaze, a servant girl recognized him in the flickering light. "You were with Jesus," she said.

"I do not know what you mean," Peter said.

Another servant girl noticed him. "This man was with Jesus of Nazareth," she said to those around her.

"I was not," Peter said.

"Certainly, you too are one of them," some bystanders said. "Your accent betrays you."

"I do not know the man!" Peter insisted.

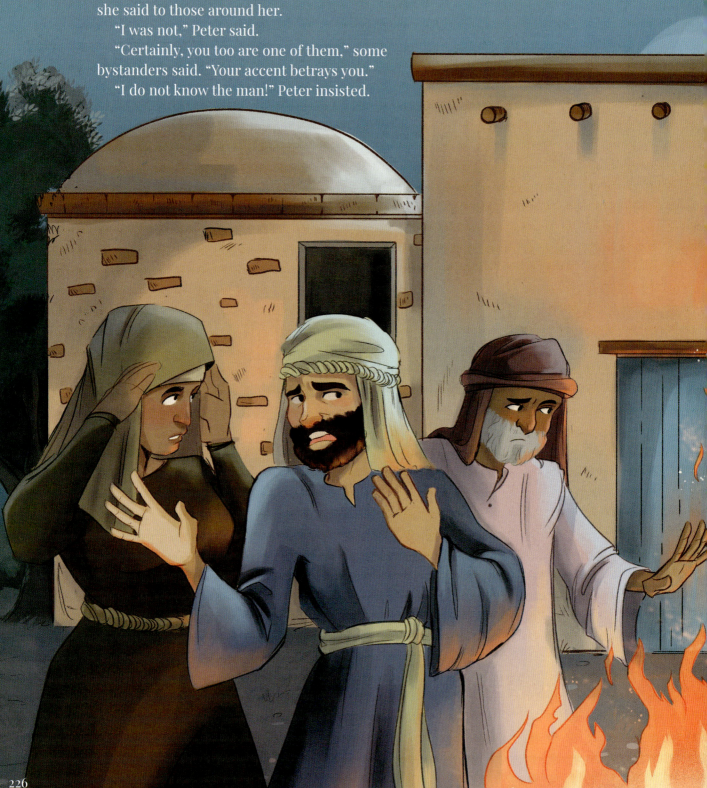

Then the rooster crowed—*COCK-A-DOODLE-DOO!* Jesus turned and met Peter's eyes.

Can you imagine the sorrow in His gaze?

Peter had denied Jesus three times, exactly as the Lord had predicted. Upon realizing his betrayal, Peter ran out and wept bitterly.

Meanwhile, the chief priests and scribes dragged Jesus before their high priest, Caiaphas, and called witnesses to accuse Him. One person after another spoke lies about Jesus, but their stories contradicted each other. Finally, Caiaphas stood up. "By the living God, tell us if you are the Christ, the Son of God," he demanded.

Jesus said to them, "You have said so." And then He quoted the prophet Daniel: "But from now on the Son of Man shall be seated at the right hand of the power of God and coming on the clouds of heaven." Jesus was declaring that *He* was the Son of Man, equal to God.

Upon hearing this, Caiaphas tore his robes. "What further testimony do we need? You have heard his blasphemy!" he cried.

"He deserves death!" the council shouted, and they spat in Jesus's face and struck Him. Then they brought Him before Pontius Pilate, the Roman governor of Judea, and demanded Jesus's execution.

Pilate didn't find Jesus guilty of anything, but the mob cried out in rage. To appease them, Pilate ordered his soldiers to whip Jesus. Soldiers beat Jesus, put a purple robe on Him, and twisted together a crown of thorns for His head. Then they mocked Him and cried out, "Hail, King of the Jews!"

Afterward, Pilate brought Jesus before the crowd again, the purple robe still hanging about His shoulders and blood staining the ground where He stood. "Behold the man!" Pilate said.

"Crucify him! Crucify him!" the crowd shouted. What horror! The very people Jesus came to save now cried out against Him. They demanded Pilate's soldiers nail Jesus to a wooden cross and abandon Him to die while onlookers jeered.

"Shall I crucify your King?" Pilate asked.

"We have no king but Caesar!" the chief priests said. "Crucify him, and release Barabbas in his place." Barabbas was a murderer, locked in prison for fighting against Rome. He would go free, while the Son of God, who had never sinned, would die.

Pilate gave in. He washed his hands to symbolize his innocence in Jesus's death. And he turned Jesus—the Christ, the Messiah, the Savior of the world—over for crucifixion.

- Could Jesus have saved Himself if He had wanted to? Why didn't He?

More of the Story—Read Isaiah 53:7. How did Jesus fulfill this verse?

Read Deuteronomy 21:22–23, which says that people hung on a tree (put to death by being nailed to a cross) were cursed by God. Discuss with a grown-up the significance of Jesus's crucifixion.

Illustrations by Evelt Yanait

32

The Darkest Day

Psalm 22; Matthew 27:27-66; Luke 23:44-56; John 19

God's own Son, who was with God at the very beginning, stumbled along in chains. He had the power to command the seas, but now He stooped and bled, falling under the weight of the cross He carried, the cross to which soldiers would soon nail Him. Couldn't He have called armies of angels to rescue Him?

What do you think?

Yes. He could have. But He suffered willingly to save you and me. To save even those who would hate Him.

The soldiers forced Jesus to a place where even the earth warned of death—a skull-shaped hill called Golgotha. There they stripped Him of His clothes, laid Him on a wooden cross, and nailed His feet and hands to the beams—just as David had prophesied, when long ago he wrote, "they have pierced my hands and feet." The soldiers lifted the cross so all would see Jesus's broken body.

Oh, what a dreadful day! How could the sun bear to show its face through the clouds as the One who created it hung upon the cross?

As Jesus hung there betrayed and battered, do you think He slung insults at His captors? Did He curse them or call down fire from heaven?

Oh no, dear friend. Instead He spoke these words: "Father, forgive them, for they know not what they do."

The soldiers crucified Jesus between two criminals who also hung on crosses. One of the criminals yelled at Jesus. "Are you not the Christ?" he screeched. "Save yourself and us!"

"Do you not fear God?" the other man said. "We are receiving the due reward of our deeds, but this man has done nothing wrong." He turned toward Jesus. "Remember me when you come into your kingdom," he said.

Even now, moments before death, Jesus overflowed with compassion. "Truly, I say to you," He said, "today you will be with me in paradise."

Meanwhile, crowds gathered below. Some wept. Others mocked. "He saved others, but he cannot save himself!" the chief priests, scribes, and elders scoffed. "He trusts in God; let God deliver him now." They spoke the same words David, so long ago, had prophesied would come from the mouths of the Messiah's enemies.

The soldiers divided His clothing among themselves and cast lots to decide who should have it. Just as David, so long ago, had predicted people would do to the Messiah.

Finally, the sun's light failed. Although it was only afternoon, all the land became dark. Centuries before, darkness covered Egypt before the deaths of its firstborn sons; now darkness again cloaked the land before the death of God's own firstborn Son.

As the shadow passed over the land, Jesus called out, "My God, my God, why have you forsaken me?" Just as David, so long ago, had prophesied about the Messiah.

Jesus cried out again with a loud voice, "Father, into your hands I commit my spirit!" And with these words, God's one and only Son died.

As Jesus's last breath mingled with the air, the earth itself shook and shuddered. Rocks split wide open with a *CRACK!* The curtain of the temple, which for centuries separated people from God's holy presence, ripped in two from top to bottom, as if a great hand from heaven had torn it. "Truly, this man was the Son of God!" said a centurion as the ground shook beneath him.

A good and righteous man named Joseph of Arimathea took Jesus's body, wrapped it in a linen cloth, laid it in a tomb cut from stone, and sealed the entrance with a great rock. The chief priests ordered soldiers to guard the tomb day and night, to ensure no one took Jesus's body. Inside, the Savior of the world, God's own Son, lay for three days in darkness and silence.

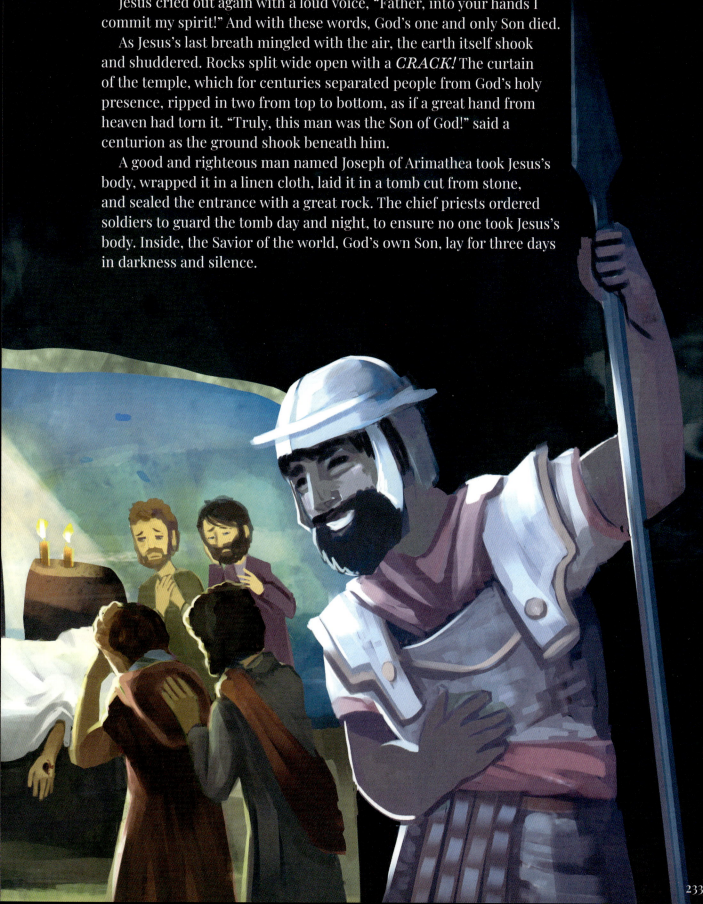

But the Light of the world would not lie there forever.

- The criminal placed his faith in Jesus at the very last moment, and Jesus promised he'd enter heaven. What hope do His words give you?

- On the cross, Jesus took the punishment all of us deserve. How does God's forgiveness change your life?

More of the Story—Read Psalm 22 with a grown-up, and together count all the ways Jesus's crucifixion fulfills this prophecy.

To whom can you tell this story today?

Illustrations by Mira Miroslavova

33

The Empty Tomb

Matthew 28:1–10; Luke 24:1–12; John 20:1–18

For three days, Jesus lay in the silence and darkness of the tomb. The sun set on Friday evening, rose Saturday morning, and set Saturday evening again. In the gray light before dawn on Sunday, the Son of God still drew no breath.

At the Pharisees' and Sadducees' request, Pilate ordered soldiers to stand at the entrance to the tomb. The scribes and priests remembered Jesus's remarks about the sign of Jonah, and they wanted to ensure His disciples didn't steal His body and claim He'd risen from the dead. For two nights, the soldiers stood guard. For two nights, nothing happened.

Then dawn broke on the third day.

As sunlight spilled over the horizon, an earthquake shook the ground! An angel suddenly appeared, bright as lightning and in clothes as white as snow. He rolled away the stone at the entrance to the tomb, and the guards trembled and fell motionless to the ground.

Meanwhile, some of Jesus's women disciples, including one named Mary Magdalene, went to the tomb to prepare His body with spices.

Imagine their terror when they found the stone rolled away from the tomb entrance and an angel awaiting them! "Do not be afraid," the angel said, "for I know you seek Jesus who was crucified. He is not here, for he has risen. Come, see the place where he lay."

When the women peered into the dark tomb, looking for the body of their beloved Lord, they found only the linen burial cloths folded by themselves. Jesus had vanished!

What had happened? Where was Jesus's body?

Mary lingered outside the tomb and wept. First, she'd watched Jesus die on the cross; now His body had disappeared. How could this be?

Then she turned around and saw a man standing behind her. *It must be the gardener*, she thought. *Perhaps he'll know what's happened to my Lord.*

"Woman, why are you weeping?" the man asked. "Whom are you seeking?"

"Sir, if you have carried my Lord away, tell me where you have laid him. I will take him," Mary said.

"Mary."

Perhaps it was His voice, the unmistakable tone she treasured in her mind. Perhaps it was the way He said her name. Perhaps He'd just opened her eyes, and suddenly she could see what she had been blind to moments before. Whatever the reason, suddenly, immediately, wonderfully, Mary knew.

This man was no gardener. He was the risen Lord!

Can you imagine how her heart burst? He was alive! The Savior, God's own Son, was alive! "Teacher!" Mary cried, perhaps rushing toward Him with outstretched arms.

"Do not cling to me, Mary, for I have not yet ascended to the Father," Jesus said. "Instead, go to my brothers and say to them, 'I am ascending to my Father and your Father, to my God and your God.'"

Mary raced to obey Him. Tears must have streaked down her face, and her heart must have raced as she ran. When she found the disciples, the words must have leaped from her throat like a river bursting through a dam: "I have seen the Lord!" she cried.

He is risen—hallelujah!

More of the Story—Jesus's resurrection surprised the disciples . . . but did it surprise Jesus? Hint: read Matthew 17:22.

Read John 11:25 and 1 Corinthians 15:22. What promise do we have now that Jesus has risen from the dead?

Jesus didn't come on a war horse, but He won the greatest battle of all. What was that battle? Hint: read 2 Timothy 1:10.

To whom can you tell this story today?

Illustrations by Sayada Ramdial

Into the Clouds

Matthew 28:16–20; Luke 24:36–53; John 20:19–29; Acts 1:6–11; 1 Corinthians 15:3–7

When Mary breathlessly told the disciples she had seen Jesus alive again, at first they didn't believe her. Some of them had seen Jesus breathe His last with their own eyes. How could He possibly be alive? They still didn't understand that this mystery, this wonder, had been God's plan all along. The prophets had predicted that God's own Son would pay the penalty for our sins and then rise to life again. But the disciples' eyes could not yet see, and their minds could not yet understand. And so, instead of celebrating, they hid from the Pharisees behind locked doors.

While they huddled, Jesus suddenly appeared among them! "Peace to you!" He said.

The disciples jumped in fright. *It's a ghost!* they all thought.

"Why are you troubled, and why do doubts arise in your hearts?" Jesus said. "See my hands and my feet, that it is I myself. Touch me and see. For a spirit does not have flesh and bones as you see that I have." Then He showed them His hands and His feet, still marked from where nails had pierced them. "Peace be with you. As the Father has sent me, even so I am sending you."

They marveled at Him, their hearts swelling with joy but their minds frozen in disbelief. Finally, to fully convince them, He asked for something to eat. They gave Him a piece of broiled fish, and He ate it before them. This was no ghost!

"I told you that everything written about me in the Law of Moses and the Prophets and the Psalms must be fulfilled," Jesus said. Then He opened their minds to understand the Scriptures. All the events—His arrest, His crucifixion, and now His resurrection from the dead—were part of God's great, beautiful story.

The Savior who would crush the head of the serpent had to live the life we should have lived and die the death we all deserved. Jesus had paid the price for our sins. He'd secured us a life with God not for a time, but *forever*. He had given His life so that all who repent of their sins and place their faith in Him will live with God for eternity.

Finally, at long last, after so many generations, He had broken the curse. God had kept His promise. Jesus had done it!

Over the next forty days, Jesus cared for and taught His disciples. He walked by the shore while Peter fished on the Sea of Galilee, and on His command the fishing nets burst with multitudes of wriggling fish, just as they had when Jesus first called Peter as a disciple. Jesus appeared to five hundred people all at once. Finally, He spoke to His disciples on a mountaintop and told them to tell this story to everyone, everywhere. "All authority in heaven and on earth has been given to me. Go therefore and make disciples of all nations, baptizing them in the name of the Father and of the Son and of the Holy Spirit, teaching them to observe all I have commanded you. And behold, I am with you always, to the end of the age."

Every nation and every person, those in the dry deserts to the lush rainforests to the windswept highlands, needed to hear God's story—to hear the story of what Jesus had done for them!

But how could the disciples possibly reach so many people? And what did Jesus mean, that He would always be with them?

Before the disciples could ask questions, Jesus lifted His hands and blessed them. Then He was carried up into heaven and vanished within the clouds.

As the disciples stood gazing after Him, their faces tipped heavenward, two men in white robes appeared before them. "Men of Galilee, why do you stand looking into heaven?" the angels said. "This Jesus, who was taken up from you into heaven, will come in the same way as you saw him go."

The disciples praised God and returned to Jerusalem rejoicing. Jesus had risen. He had risen, indeed!

- The good news of Jesus's death and resurrection is called the gospel. How would you summarize the gospel if you were to tell it to others?

- How does knowing that Jesus died for your sins, and that through faith in Him you have eternal life, change your view of life?

More of the Story—The apostle Paul says that through Jesus, "death is swallowed up in victory" (1 Corinthians 15:55). What hope does this verse give you?

To whom can you tell this story today?

Illustrations by Alida Massari

35

Tongues of Flame

John 14:25–31; 15:26–27; Acts 2; Romans 8:38–39; Revelation 21:4

Once Jesus had returned to heaven, the apostles all gathered together in one place and marveled at the teachings of their Lord. Jesus had told them to tell everyone what they had seen and to spread the message throughout all the earth . . . but how? During the Last Supper, Jesus had promised He would send the Holy Spirit—the same Spirit that so mysteriously descended upon Him in the form of a dove at His baptism—to help the apostles retell all they'd seen and heard. Where was this Helper? When would He come? How could they tell the story to all the nations when they knew so little beyond their own homelands?

What do you think?

While the disciples gathered, a sound like a mighty wind suddenly rushed down from heaven, filling the entire house. Before their eyes, tongues of flickering flame appeared and rested atop each one of them. It was the Holy Spirit—the Helper Jesus had promised! In an instant, all the disciples began to speak clearly in languages they'd never studied! They spoke the languages of Egypt and Libya, Mesopotamia and Asia, Crete and Arabia, Rome, and every nation under heaven.

The apostles' speech drew crowds, as people in Jerusalem who'd traveled from distant lands recognized their own languages. "Aren't these people who are speaking Galileans?" they asked in astonishment. "How is it that we hear them telling the mighty works of God in our own tongues?" God had undone the destruction of Babel! Long ago, mankind's pride had scattered the nations, but with the help of the Spirit, God's story would unite them again.

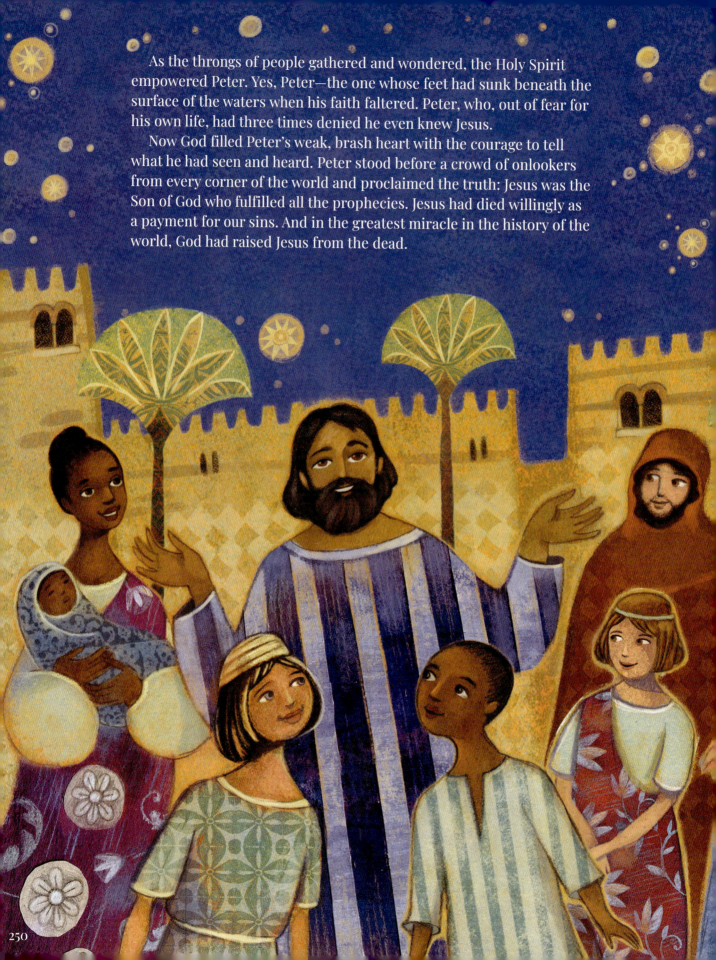

As the throngs of people gathered and wondered, the Holy Spirit empowered Peter. Yes, Peter—the one whose feet had sunk beneath the surface of the waters when his faith faltered. Peter, who, out of fear for his own life, had three times denied he even knew Jesus.

Now God filled Peter's weak, brash heart with the courage to tell what he had seen and heard. Peter stood before a crowd of onlookers from every corner of the world and proclaimed the truth: Jesus was the Son of God who fulfilled all the prophecies. Jesus had died willingly as a payment for our sins. And in the greatest miracle in the history of the world, God had raised Jesus from the dead.

When the crowd heard this, at first they became upset. Their leaders had demanded Jesus's crucifixion. Some of the people may have even called for it themselves. Jesus truly was the promised Messiah—and yet, they'd killed Him! How could they carry on?

"Brothers, what shall we do?" they cried to the apostles.

"Repent and be baptized every one of you in the name of Jesus Christ for the forgiveness of your sins, and you will receive the gift of the Holy Spirit," Peter assured them. "For the promise is for you and for your children and for all who are far off, everyone whom the Lord our God calls to himself."

At Peter's words, awe touched every soul. Jesus had died for them all! He'd died for people *everywhere*, and all those who placed their faith in Him had forgiveness—forgiveness, and the promise of eternal life! Jesus would one day return to bring a new heaven and a new earth, and He would wipe away every tear from every eye. Through faith in Jesus, nothing ever again could separate people from God's love.

Three thousand people heard Peter's words that day and believed. Soon the story of God's goodness and mercy—the story of His Savior—spread to every corner of the earth. God had promised Abraham his descendants would outnumber the stars, and God fulfilled that promise through Jesus, as the people saved through Him numbered in the thousands and millions. His story spread to Asia and the Americas, to Australia and Africa. It spread to cities and fortresses, towns and villages. It spread to fathers and grandfathers, mothers and daughters.

And to children like you.

This is the greatest story in the history of the world. It's a story *for you*. And it's a wondrous story, because when you share it, it changes lives and hearts.

To whom can you tell this story today?

Illustrations by Carlos Vélez Aguilera

Ten Tips for Reading Aloud

Children naturally delight in stories. So when you crack the spine of a book and pull up a chair, chances are they will gather around. In the best scenarios, they'll lean in with their imaginations afire in anticipation of the next surprise or delight as you read. However, we live and labor in a broken world, replete with dinging phones, sniffly noses, and flies that buzz and draw young gazes toward the ceiling. If you find read-aloud time more clumsy than idyllic, the following tips may help recapture the wonder of God's story for the children in your life.

Put away the electronic devices.

Studies show that interruptions from cell phones diminish children's learning during parent-child interactions.[1] In an era when smartphones and tablets have morphed into appendages, putting all devices away and devoting ten minutes exclusively to reading offers kids a rare gift. Not only are you modeling behavior beneficial to their development, but you're also sending the message that reading about God's story is *important*—so important that all interruptions can wait.

Embrace the wonder.

God's story is wonderful. Embrace the wonder! Enjoy this time sharing the good news with kids. Approach the task enthusiastically. Delight in God's astounding love and mercy, which He so exquisitely expresses through Christ. When you approach reading as an exercise in joy, you'll stir up your listeners' excitement too.

Slow down.

Take your time reading stories. Read slowly and clearly so kids can linger over the words. Children vary in their abilities to develop mental pictures in response to a story; ensure you've given your listeners time to wrap their minds around the images and the action.

---

[1] Jessa Reed, Kathy Hirsh-Pasek, and Roberta Michnick Golinkoff, "Learning on Hold: Cell Phones Sidetrack Parent-Child Interactions," *Developmental Psychology* 53, no. 8 (2017): 1428-1436. https://templeinfantlab.com/wp-content/uploads/sites/2/2017/12/Learning-on-Hold.pdf (Accessed April 20, 2024).

Read with expression.

Don't just recite—tantalize! In contrast to expository writing, stories invite theatrical readings. Vary your speed and rhythm. Play around with lively voices for each character—even silly ones if appropriate!

Add sound effects.

Many children's stories—including some of those in this book—feature words that mimic specific sounds. Make use of these moments to bring the story alive.

Don't be afraid to move!

Don't feel pressured to include sophisticated choreography into your story time, but carefully timed motions can help stories come alive for listeners. Stomp when the characters stomp! Duck down when they hide! Mimic David whipping his sling through the air!

Use pauses wisely.

Children's stories often include familiar or repeated lines. In such instances, pause before predictable words and engage listeners in the story by inviting them to answer. Also pause to give listeners time to wonder what will happen next. Time these pauses carefully, as too many can break up the flow of the story. Use pauses to enhance their experience, not detract from it.

Show the pictures.

If possible, when reading to a group, hold the book to the side of your face as you read, with the pages displayed outward. If this is uncomfortable or awkward, read with expression, and then after reading a page sweep the book in front of you, pages out, so everyone can examine the illustrations.

Don't stress about age or grade level.

Kids' listening comprehension often exceeds their reading comprehension. Don't worry about a story being "above" kids' heads. They will often understand more than you expect, especially when there are pictures to help tell the story. And if you're open and inviting, kids will speak up if a vocabulary word confuses them. Additionally, often-surly older kids are sometimes more open to listening to books than we anticipate!

Make it a routine.

Introduce something new, and kids may grumble. Make reading aloud a habit, however, and children come to cherish the time as part of their routine. The "right" time to read is the time that's most reliably convenient—after Sunday school; during lunch, when munching kids are a captive audience; or in the darkening minutes before bed. Incorporate reading into the routine with your young ones, and watch their excitement as the time draws near for another story.

Illustrations by Thanos Tsilis

Pointing Children to the Gospel Through Great Stories

Bible stories offer obvious riches to families, inspiring children to harbor God's truth in their hearts even as they delight in the vibrancy and wonder of a well-wrought narrative. But what do we make of all the *other* titles that clutter children's bookshelves? How do we approach the tomes with worn spines and dog-eared pages that tantalize our kids but say nothing overt about the greatest story of all?

Don't toss out the secular books just yet. No fiction can replace God's inspired Word, but the right stories—those that celebrate goodness in the face of wickedness, hope in the darkness, and whatever is just, true, and lovely (Philippians 4:8)—can help point our kids to the one, true story of Christ crucified and risen for us.[1] Reading aloud, in addition to all its neurodevelopmental and social-emotional benefits, offers a golden opportunity to discuss biblical truths—even when those truths don't explicitly parade through the text.

I first glimpsed the power of great stories to enrich gospel teaching while reading *The Fellowship of the Ring* with my kids. My son and daughter munched peanut butter and jelly sandwiches while Frodo and his companions fled across the bridge of Khazad-dûm. As Gandalf wheeled about to face the Balrog, my kids paused mid-bite and leaned in, enraptured. The bridge gave way; my kids leaned in farther. Then the Balrog's whip lashed around Gandalf's ankle. The beloved wizard urged the fellowship to save themselves, and then he sank into the abyss.

I paused and studied my kids warily. Was this too much? Would their sensitive minds buckle under the tragedy of this scene?

I held my breath as my son finally spoke up. "I think he gave himself for the others, Mum," he said. "Kind of like Jesus did for us."

Great stories like Tolkien's offer beautiful opportunities to discuss gospel truths, even when the text doesn't mention Jesus's name. Sarah Mackenzie says, "When we read a story with our children that is true—not in a literal sense, but in the supernatural sense—we don't close a book and say, 'And that is how it happened, exactly like that.' We say, rather, *'There he is.'* Because truth always, always leads us back to gazing heavenward."[2]

---

[1] Adapted from the author's article, "Point Kids to the Gospel Through Great Books," which originally appeared on The Gospel Coalition blog on January 10, 2020: https://www.thegospelcoalition.org/article/point-kids-gospel-great-books/ (Accessed April 22, 2024).

[2] Sarah Mackenzie, *The Read-Aloud Family: Making Meaningful and Lasting Connections with Your Kids* (Grand Rapids: Zondervan, 2018), 54.

How do we harness this power of stories to point kids heavenward in an era when ideas counter to Christianity have woven themselves into every avenue of our culture? How do we guard their minds and hearts when libraries proudly display books that denigrate the biblical worldview? The following suggestions may help you steer kids toward books reflective of Philippians 4:8, toward books that are true, honorable, just, pure, lovely, and commendable. Such books, featuring beautiful language and themes of courage, sacrifice, and compassion, can inspire dinner-table discussions about our Savior, from whom all virtues spring.

Give them Scripture first.

The gospel will come alive through great books only if kids already know the Scriptures. Give them the Bible first, foremost, and regularly. Then—and only then!—use literature as a supplement. The goal is to enhance your family devotions, not to replace them. Teach your kids that God's Word is a lamp to their feet and a light to their path (Psalm 119:105); then help them perceive glimmers of this truth through stories.

Practice discernment.

The call to shepherd the content of our kids' backpacks and bookshelves is a biblical one. We're to infuse our kids' moments with God's Word, teaching them when they rise, when they lie down, and when they walk in the way (Deuteronomy 6:6–7). Instruction in God's Word occurs not only on Sundays in the church pews but also daily, even hourly, including when our children read books under the covers with a flashlight at night. The goal isn't censorship or coddling; it's discipleship—to acknowledge that what our children read shapes their minds and to guide them tenderly and deliberately through that sculpting.

Seek books with pages that overflow with the true, pure, and lovely. Search for books that explore our sinful nature with humility, point to our hope in Christ with reverence, and highlight the victory of good over evil.

Know your kids.

It takes a discerning eye to present weighty themes like danger, loss, grief, and death in ways that move and educate but not terrify. Preview any book ahead of time. When possible, pick a story with which you're already familiar, so you can edit sections that would overwhelm your children. Ensure the illustrations aren't too graphic or upsetting. Kids' sensitivities vary. The best stories will challenge and inspire without causing distress.

Point them to the gospel.

As you read with your kids, be alert to biblical themes. Look for the redemptive arc in each story—the character arc or plotline that points to our salvation in Christ. Examples include Aslan giving his life to save Edmund in *The Lion, the Witch, and the Wardrobe*, Janner saving the cloven in The Wingfeather Saga, and Aragorn returning to rule over a kingdom made new in *The Return of the King*.

While these examples reflect the works of Christian authors, even less-overt literature can prove instructive if approached with discernment. Shakespearean tragedies vividly portray the destructive power of sin. Dickens stirs us to compassion for the poor, for widows, and for orphans (Deuteronomy 10:18; James 1:27). *The Cricket in Times Square* and *Charlotte's Web* highlight love for neighbor and hope in despair. And *Robinson Crusoe* and *The Swiss Family Robinson* illustrate God's faithfulness and provision. Even the bad guys from Greek mythology can offer teachable moments: when we openly discuss the brutality and lasciviousness of Zeus, the false deity withers before the majesty, mercy, and holiness of the one true God.

In an era when accepted values daily slip further from the teachings of Christ, redemptive, inspiring, lovely books that focus on the good and the true are as vital as air. Don't neglect such treasures. Give the kids in your life the gospel through Scripture. Then come alongside them to marvel at how the very best stories thrill us because they point to Him.

Illustrations by Breezy Brookshire

After "The End"

Deuteronomy 6:6–7 depicts an approach to discipleship unbounded by church walls and Sunday school classrooms. Rather than relegating Bible study to Sundays, we're called to infuse God's Word into every moment of our children's days: "And these words that I command you today shall be on your heart. You shall teach them diligently to your children, and shall talk of them when you sit in your house, and when you walk by the way, and when you lie down and when you rise."

Such verses guide us to continue the conversations from *The Storyteller's Bible* beyond the classroom or reading nook, into our kids' moments as they wait for the school bus, get ready for bed, or stew over multiplication tables. Bible stories lay the foundation for deeper instruction in Scripture, which is "living and active" (Hebrews 4:12), "breathed out by God and profitable for teaching" (2 Timothy 3:16). When we apply God's Word to every facet of life, our children develop eyes to see and ears to hear.

So how do we weave the greatest story into kids' daily lives? The following suggestions will help you incorporate the imagery and lessons of Bible stories into the fabric of children's days.

Continue to dialogue.

Ask kids to reflect upon the Bible stories they've heard and read, and ask questions to elicit their thoughts and test their comprehension. Even better, recall those stories during memorable moments in their lives. When fears keep kids awake, remind them

that the same God who parted the Red Sea to rescue His people also holds them in the palm of His hand (Isaiah 41:10). When someone hurts them, remind them that Jesus, too, suffered persecution yet forgave His enemies (Luke 23:34). When a rainbow lights up the sky, remind them that God sealed His promise to Noah with the very same ribbons of color (Genesis 9:16).

Recognize that God's Word is relevant for kids *today*.

The presumption that children won't understand Scripture can tempt us to delay weighty discussions and Bible study until they're older, but the truth is that the Bible is relevant for kids *now*. Even when their tender minds aren't ready for lengthy expositions of doctrine, children understand the gospel. Kids face real struggles and hard decisions at school, on the playground, and during interactions with peers. They lie awake at night haunted by fears that sometimes adopt fanciful overtones but which often include a hefty dollop of reality. Every time they draw on the walls or hit a sibling or lie about a stolen lollipop, they grasp sin and their need for forgiveness. As they grow in a sin-stricken world, kids need the truth that they are loved, redeemed, and held, no matter what calamity life brings. They need the guiding light of God's Word, even when they're too young to read the words themselves.

Give kids active roles in Bible study.

Incorporate Bible study into your routine with the young people in your life—and engage them as *active* participants. Children learn by doing, rather than passively listening. Have kids look up relevant Bible passages during your study time. Ask them questions. Challenge them to think and to apply the truths of passages to scenarios they've seen in modern life. Act out scenes to help the content stick.

"Graduate" kids to the real text.

Kids thrive on repetition. Once they've read a cherished Bible story over and over, then read the corresponding chapters in the Bible. Storybooks such as this one offer excellent scaffolding for kids to comprehend and wrap their minds around the real thing. Additionally, this transition emphasizes to kids that Bible stories are *true* stories rather than myths.

Retell the story.

Prompts throughout this book encourage listeners to share the Bible stories they hear with others. Model this for your kids! Talk regularly and often about God's work through Christ. When you engage with others, share your faith—and invite the kids in your life along when you do. Prompt kids to ask themselves, "Who can I share this story with today?" Encourage them to pray about friends and loved ones who need God's Word. Peter declared he had no choice but to share what he'd seen and heard (Acts 4:20); show it's okay to do the same.

Keep the gospel central.

Too often, Bible storybooks treat Scripture as a rulebook or as a series of disjointed stories without cohesive meaning. Such an approach couldn't be further from the truth. God is a storyteller, and throughout Scripture He offers us the most beautiful story of all—how He so loved the world, that He gave His one and only Son for us (John 3:16). When discussing stories, try to connect them to the overall narrative arc of the Bible, emphasizing the reality of sin and the tremendous Good News of our salvation in Christ.

About the Artists

As gifts from the greatest Storyteller, all modes of creativity can weave stories. While the writer wields words, the illustrator uses color and imagery to bring scenes to life. These thirty-two visual storytellers from around the world used their unique talents to envision the people and places of each Bible story. The resulting diversity and richness of artwork promises to stir children's imaginations, pointing all the while to God's beautiful narrative of hope and redemption.

Monica Garofalo (Story 1; art also used on back cover and page 272) graduated in graphic design and multimedia, Master Ars In Fabula of Editorial Illustration, and works as an illustrator with clients such as Universal, Usborne, Maverick Books Warren, ReaderLink, YOYO Books, Lifeway, Insight Editions, Notes Publishers, and Giunti Editore. She lives in Trento, Italy, and teaches graphic design and animation to adults and in companies. In her work, Monica uses digital and mixes watercolor and mixed techniques to obtain colorful and fun gradations and textures in line with the ironic tone of her images.

Jade van der Zalm (Stories 2 and 10) is an illustrator and storyteller who was born in Zhanjiang, China, but grew up in the Netherlands, where she still lives. She has a deep love for stories, whether written, drawn or told! When drawing, her favorite thing is working with color and light and experimenting with all the options that gives her. Aside from drawing she loves to cook, travel, and dabble in street photography.

Sarah Horne (Story 3) learned to draw while trying to explain her reasoning for an elaborate haircut at the age of nine. She started her illustration career while freelancing for newspapers and also worked on commissions for advertising clients such as Nike, IKEA, and Kew Gardens. She has illustrated over one hundred books, including *Charlie Changes into a Chicken*, *Fizzlebert Stump: The Boy Who Ran Away from the Circus (and Joined the Library)*, *Puppy Academy*, and *Ask Oscar* and its sequels. She loves to include detail and extra visual narratives in her work. She works entirely digitally. When not at her desk in London, England, Sarah loves running, painting, photography, cooking, film, and a good stomp up a hill.

Ken Daley (Story 4) is an award-winning Black Canadian artist/illustrator who was born to parents who emigrated from Dominica. His art and illustrations are inspired by his Afro-Caribbean heritage, and he has exhibited his work in Canada, the United States, and the Caribbean. Ken has illustrated fifteen children's books and is working on five more. He has received an Américas Award and a Kirkus Best Picture Book for *Auntie Luce's Talking Paintings* and was awarded Best Illustration for *Black Boy, Black Boy*. He believes that diverse stories are essential to creating a more just and equitable world, which he's deeply committed to manifesting through his art and illustrations.

Breezy Brookshire (Story 5 and pages 262–265) is the illustrator of several children's books including *Audrey Bunny, For Such a Time as This, A Little More Beautiful: The Story of a Garden,* and *The King of All Things.* Breezy grew up in Indiana, spending her childhood drawing, exploring the outdoors, and crafting, which deeply influenced her art and love for nature. She now lives in Franklin, Tennessee.

Cornelius Van Wright (Story 6) is an award-winning children's book illustrator, an author, and an art instructor. He has illustrated numerous picture books, many of which he co-illustrated with his wife, Ying Hwa-Hu. His work has appeared on *Reading Rainbow* and *Storytime* and has been exhibited in Bologna Book Fair and the Society of Illustrators. Cornelius's authored-illustrated picture books have garnered praise from *The Horn Book, Kirkus Review, School Library Journal, Publishers Weekly, Booklist,* and many others. Cornelius also teaches at Fred Dolan Art Academy, and his students have attended and graduated from many top art colleges in the country. He lives with his wife in New York City.

Carlos Vélez Aguilera (Stories 7 and 13 and pages 254–257; art also used on back cover and page 6) was born in Mexico City and is a graduate of the National School of Plastic Arts of the National University Autonomous of Mexico. He has illustrated books for various publishers in Mexico such as: Santillana, Ediciones Castillo, Norma, SM, Trillas, Richmond, Alfaguara, and Porrua, as well as a large number of magazines and animation projects. He has illustrated more than twenty children's books as well as writing *Salón Destino.* Carlos has been recognized with two illustration awards in the catalog for the International Children's and Youth Book Fair in Mexico.

Natalie Peterson (Story 8) is an illustrator and background painter based in Nashville, Tennessee. She illustrated the children's book *We Carry Kevan* and painted backgrounds for Andrew Peterson's animated Wingfeather Saga. Her love of wonder and whimsy in the Lord's creation informs all her messy mark making. Natalie is living the dream—making art from home with her husband and little daughter in their glitter-filled office.

Thanos Tsilis (Story 9 and pages 258–261) was born and raised in Athens, Greece. From an early age, comics and cartoon animations fascinated him, and he yearned to learn how they were created. He pursued studies in graphic design, 2D animation, and illustration. He has worked on animated films, created storyboards, and illustrated numerous books, often focusing on historical themes for clients worldwide, and has dabbled in video game design. However, his true passion is creating his own graphic novels. Recently, his most substantial graphic novel was published in his country, and more are on the horizon. Thanos lives in Athens as a daddy of two kids who don't let him draw as much as he would like, but somehow he manages all his obligations nicely.

Kristi Smith (Story 11; art also used on page 7) is the illustrator of several children's books and coloring books, most worked on with her husband, Jay, at Juicebox Designs, their graphic design studio in Nashville, Tennessee. She grew up in western Texas, loving to draw, color, read constantly, and go on camping trips with her family. She studied graphic design and illustration in college, graduated with honors, and has been illustrating professionally since 1997. Inspired by music, nature, and a huge range of personal interests in art history, ancient arts and crafts, lettering, and archaeology, Kristi loves settling into a big job—with a stack of audiobooks and her sheepdog asleep at her feet—and losing herself in drawing.

Jesus Lopez (Story 12; art also used on page 7) was born in Madrid, Spain. From a very young age, he loved to draw, often by copying superheroes from comics and inventing new characters. He studied cinema at a film academy in Madrid and made several short films. Since 2000 he has worked as a freelance illustrator for several European publishers. His great passions are drawing, cinema, nature, and his little daughter, Paula. He always works while listening to something, most of the time to podcasts of film, art, history, or music. He loves film soundtracks, Bob Dylan, and pop rock of the 70s and 80s. Jesus currently lives with his family in a small town 50 kilometers from Madrid. When he is not drawing, he loves going to the cinema, walking in nature, and playing with his daughter.

Matt Forsyth (Story 14) started his working life as a commercial banker running projects in process management. This pathway in the seemingly wrong direction gave him valuable skills in managing a client's project from start to finish and ensuring its completion in a timely manner. He then went on to work as a lead artist in the games industry. After that he worked for the Navy and Air Force creating 3D training videos to cover a wide range of topics. Matt now freelances for wonderfully varied clients, from indie games companies and virtual supermarkets to children's book publishers. He lives in Auckland, New Zealand.

Evelline Andrya (Story 15; art also used on page 7) was born in Sumatra, Indonesia, as a Chinese-Javanese. She grew up in the Equatorial Emerald, the country of 17,000 islands. Her life is surrounded by the diversity of Indonesian culture—colorful tribes, tropical rainforest and wildlife, underwater paradise, historical marvels—that became the influence for her vibrant artwork. Evelline currently lives in Java with her husband, their four children, and a fluffy Pomeranian.

Mark Cowden (Story 16) has been creating art for over thirty years and holds a BFA degree from the University of Tennessee. He works primarily as an oil painter, exploring a variety of genres including landscape, portraiture, and figurative art as well as creating mosaic art, sculpture, and large-scale public art installations and murals. His inspiration comes from a variety of places—a doodle at the family dinner table, an encounter with someone, or scenery from places he longs to visit. Constant creative exploration is key to maintaining excitement and integrity in his work. Mark is also an award-winning graphic designer and creative director for B&H Publishing, creating books and marketing and publicity materials for authors. He can often be found working in his home studio with his wife and fellow artist Yvette Renée in Hendersonville, Tennessee.

Alisha Monnin (Story 17; art also used on page 2) was born and raised in rural Ohio in a small village where distance is measured by cornfields. Growing up, she was a voracious reader and daydreamed about going on magical adventures. As an adult, she still does! Alisha graduated from the Savannah College of Art and Design and now resides in Cincinnati, Ohio, with her Manx cat, Beignet.

Wazza Pink (Story 18; art also used on back cover) is an illustrator based in her beloved hometown of Hanoi, Vietnam, from which she gets her creative inspiration. Most of her illustrations are made for and deal with kids—their youthful innocence, playfulness, purity of soul, and curious gazes. For every piece of art, she favors a multi-dimensional and gentle approach through which she can truly feel the whole spirit of an art theme, thereby being able to grasp the ideas and convey them into a sketch.

César Samaniego (Story 19) was born in Barcelona, Spain. He grew up smelling his father's oils, reading his comic books, and trying to paint over his illustrations (he was so happy to see the way he could improve his father's work). But César didn't realize that he wanted to be an illustrator himself until he met his wife. He then went to Llotja Arts and Crafts School and graduated with honors. Since then, he has published many books and app books, worked on textbooks for schools and as a layout artist for animation. He and his wife also have their own children's clothes trademark. César now lives in Canet de Mar, a small town on the coast of Barcelona, with his wife, his daughter, five cats, and a crazy dog.

Clara Anganuzzi (Story 20) would draw on every single surface she could find (including some very unhappy tortoises) while growing up in the Seychelles. She always had a fond love for animals and creating characters with subtle, gentle humor. Using a mixture of traditional techniques, ranging from monoprint to pencil, Clara enjoys creating narratives and images with a sense of place in limited color palettes. After finishing her BA illustration degree at Falmouth University, she went on to complete an MA in children's illustration at Anglia Ruskin University, which helped her gain inspiration and motivation as well as showcase her personal voice. Clara lives in Bristol, England.

Aedan Peterson (Story 21) is an illustrator and visual developer born and raised in Nashville, Tennessee. He's been jumping between the publishing and animation worlds for the last few years and really enjoys just getting to draw stuff for work. When he's not painting trees with his wife or playing with his daughter, he can be found birdwatching, eating chips and salsa, or doing both at the same time.

Evelt Yanait (Stories 22 and 32) is a freelance children's illustrator from Barcelona, Spain. With a passion for learning, she pursued degrees in Journalism and Social Education, and added postgraduate studies in Creativity & Advertising and Graphic Design to her portfolio. For many years, Evelt has brought stories to life through her illustrations, working on board games and children's books for clients around the world, and writing her own stories too. Beyond her art, Evelt loves to write, travel, and watch documentaries, always on the lookout for new stories and lifestyles to capture. She loves people. She has a keen interest in education, with a special focus on emotional intelligence.

Mariano Epelbaum (Story 23) is an illustrator and character designer from Buenos Aires, Argentina. He enjoys trying different styles of illustration, as he is inspired by each project he works on. Mariano worked as art director and character designer on the animated 3D movie *Underdogs*. He has published books in the United States, Spain, Argentina, England, Mexico, and Puerto Rico. When he's not working, he likes playing with his two daughters, watching movies, and going for outdoor walks.

James Bernardin (Story 24) creates illustrations that travel the creative realm between whimsy and realism, with off-ramps to history, folklore, fantasy, and early childhood. This journey has allowed him to create artwork for many children's picture books, middle-grade novels, book covers, magazines, TV commercials, trading cards, and major advertising campaigns. James has been recognized by the Society of Illustrators and praised by numerous book reviewers, and he has been the recipient of two Telly awards. Trained in traditional and digital mediums, James graduated with honors from ArtCenter College of Design in California. He calls Poulsbo, Washington, home these days, where he lives with his wife and two sons.

Arief Putra (Story 25) was born on Borneo Island in Indonesia and spent his childhood living at the edge of a rainforest. After leaving a career in architecture to pursue his true passion of storytelling illustration, Arief has been working on several projects from international publishers. He works from his small rural home in Yogyakarta City where he lives with his wife and two sons. He also enjoys fresh ground morning coffee, weekend cooking, space documentaries, and solving the Rubik's Cube.

Patrick Corrigan (Story 26) is an illustrator and author who grew up in a cloudy town in Cheshire, where he brightened up his life with various creative endeavors and activities (his favorite was cross-stitch!). He studied ceramics at university before training as an art teacher. He then went on to become the art director of a busy design studio in London. In 2018 he made the decision to try his hand as a freelance illustrator and has never looked back. His work has been commissioned by numerous clients, including Walker, Flying Eye Books, HarperCollins, Penguin, Hachette, and Quarto. He lives in Cheshire, United Kingdom.

Diana Lawrence (Story 27) is the art director and designer of this book and many others by B&H Publishing. She grew up drawing, treasuring a storybook with each tale illustrated by a different artist—so sharing the work of many artists in *The Storyteller's Bible* is the realization of a long-held dream! After studying graphic design and illustration, she began work as an advertising artist then moved to publication design. She has designed all genres of literature for more than thirty years and delights most in creating expressions of God's love for children through the wonder of art and story. She also makes mixed-media pieces with seashells gathered on the Outer Banks of North Carolina where she lives.

Ana Latese (Story 28) is an African American illustrator and character designer from Raleigh, North Carolina, who enjoys producing beautiful imagery inspired by vibrant colors, fantasy elements, and joy. Ana has worked with clients such as *The Washington Post*, Penguin Random House, Hulu, and Scholastic. When she's not illustrating, she loves to play video games, drink a nice cup of tea, or play with her furry studio assistant, Jin.

Leo Trinidad (Story 29) is a *New York Times* best-selling comic book artist, illustrator, and animator from Costa Rica. He is known for being the creator of the first animated series ever produced in Central America, an outstanding achievement that led him to the foundation of Rocket Cartoons, one of the most successful animation studios in Latin America. In 2018 he won first place in the Central American Graphic Novel contest, organized by the French Alliance of Costa Rica. Moved by his love for good books, his wife, and his little girl, Emma, Leo is always bouncing between children's books, animation, and comics, and his work is constantly developing with a strong focus on storytelling.

Chiara Fedele (Story 30) was born in Milan, Italy, and now lives with her family and pets in a little village called Tromello. Chiara attended art school in Milan and took a degree in illustration at La Scuola del Fumetto in Milan. She loves bright colors and contrast and uses a combination of mixed traditional media and digital. Her artwork is varied, and she feels her style is always evolving. Expressionism is her favorite art period, and she has a particular love for the works of John Singer Sargent, Henri de-Toulouse-Lautrec, and Egon Schiele. Chiara teaches illustration and painting techniques at the International School of Comics in Brescia and Padova.

Monique Steele (Story 31) is a Jamaican-born illustrator currently residing in the small pocket of reality in between time and space (also known as Miami, Florida). Thematically, her art explores historical costuming, fan culture, and diabolical women in power. When she's not drawing famous queens in history, you can find Monique deeply mired in the comings and goings of pop culture, trying to refine her spicy foods palette, and lamenting no longer living the "island girl" lifestyle.

Mira Miroslavova (Story 33) is an award-winning children's book illustrator who grew up in the beautiful forests near Sofia, Bulgaria, where she still lives. She has studied textile arts in Manchester, United Kingdom, and her work for *The Brothers Grimm Fairy Tales* was a finalist at the Bologna Children's Book Fair in 2021. Her inspiration comes from the classic fairy tales her parents read to her as a child, united with a mixture of classic textile art and pattern designs and the modern look of freely pencil-drawn style and characters.

Sayada Ramdial (Story 34) is a freelance illustrator from Trinidad and Tobago who now lives in the Pacific Northwest with her husband and their cat. When she's not experimenting at the drawing board or in the kitchen, Sayada enjoys gardening, exploring nature, and meeting friendly, furry pets.

Alida Massari (Story 35; art also used on front cover and pages 1, 4, and 271) was born in Rome where she qualified in art at the high school and then went on to complete a specialization in illustration at the European Institute of Design. She has loved art from a young age. She finds inspiration for her work from the folk traditions and ancient art; her work is "modern but with ancient atmosphere." She has illustrated over sixty books as well as advent calendars, posters, novel covers, boardgames, and greeting cards, collaborating with Italian, English, French, German, and American publishers. Since 2020 she has been a lecturer of illustration at Rome University of Fine Art. Alida lives near Rome and has taken part in many collective illustration exhibitions in Italy and abroad.

About the Author

Christie Butler

Kathryn Butler (MD, Columbia University) is a trauma surgeon who left practice at Massachusetts General Hospital to homeschool her kids. She now writes regularly for Desiring God, The Gospel Coalition, and other ministries on the topics of faith, medicine, and the power of stories, and she's authored many books, including the middle-grade series The Dream Keeper Saga. Kathryn lives in the woods in northern Massachusetts with her husband, two kids, and two cats with Beatrix Potter-inspired names. When not writing articles and books out of joy for the Lord, she delights in leisurely hikes, strong coffee, vivid stories, and laughing out loud with her family.